Oct. 2, 2018

To my Surfside

This book if by an author ...... .om

I have grown up with in Oregon. I was

here for a retreat this weekend and

brought a few books to share.

life

as a

prayer

I hope you find peace and
strength by the sea as I did.
What a magical place to renew

HOPE LYDA

and be still.

Blessings from your neighbor

in 105.

Jackie
S.

HARVEST HOUSE PUBLISHERS
EUGENE, OREGON

LIFE AS A PRAYER
Copyright © 2009/2017 Hope Lyda
Published by Harvest House Publishers
Eugene, Oregon 97402
www.harvesthousepublishers.com

ISBN 978-0-7369-6191-2 (pbk.)
ISBN 978-0-7369-6192-9 (eBook)

Library of Congress Cataloging-in-Publication Data

Names: Lyda, Hope, author.
Title: Life as a prayer / Hope Lyda.
Description: Eugene Oregon : Harvest House Publishers, [2017]
Identifiers: LCCN 2016042141 (print) | LCCN 2016046702 (ebook) | ISBN
    9780736961912 (pbk.) | ISBN 9780736961929 (ebook)
Subjects: LCSH: Spiritual life—Christianity. | Prayer—Christianity. |
    Spiritual exercises.
Classification: LCC BV4501.3 .L95 2017 (print) | LCC BV4501.3 (ebook) | DDC
    248.3/2—dc23
LC record available at https://lccn.loc.gov/2016042141

17 18 19 20 21 22 23 24 25 / BP-GL / 10 9 8 7 6 5 4 3 2

Contents

Prayer:
Breathe It.
Live It.
Be It.

Life as a Prayer

"Why must people kneel down to pray? If I really wanted
to pray I'll tell you what I'd do. I'd go out into a great big
field all alone or into the deep, deep, woods, and I'd look
up into the sky—up—up—up—into that lovely blue sky
that looks as if there was no end to its blueness.
And then I'd just FEEL a prayer."

Lucy Maud Montgomery, *Anne of Green Gables*

How's your prayer life?"

When I hear someone say this, first I hope they aren't talking to me. Then my imagination and sense of humor team up and I envision myself existing in some parallel life where I wear a white frock, cinched in the middle with a satin sash, and go about my day enshrouded in a holy mist as I shop for cat food, scrub my bathroom floor, and emit prayers for world peace. This isn't real. (And I know it isn't real because I'm cleaning my floors.) In my journey of talking to God, however, I have experienced something that *is* real. Life is a prayer. All of life. Every moment is an invitation to experience God.

How have you encountered or lived out prayer in the past? How about now? Do you bow your head and kneel? Do you wait until you're in sanctuaries or seated in pews to pray? Do you lace up worn hiking boots and head for the trail to have your most intimate conversations with the Creator? Is prayer still an ethereal idea that hasn't yet taken on flesh and substance in your day-to-day existence?

As a shy kid who spent a good amount of time mulling over ideas and wandering the rooms of my mind, I was smitten with a God who is always available for talks and who is not only attentive but also creative about capturing *my* attention. I'd view situations through the lens of "God is in this" or "God is with me." Even when I wasn't sure about myself, I was certain of God's presence. As I got older, I kept the dialogue going with God. Though, I know there were seasons when I did more talking than listening.

> Every moment is an invitation to experience God.

The big shift in how I view prayer happened when I accompanied my husband through a long health journey. Initially I prayed frequently and fervently over decisions and for healing, resolution, next steps, and insight. But as months in the trenches of the unknown turned into years, speaking the same prayers added to the weariness. I found myself saying "Ditto" as my prayer because I had nothing new to take to God. The needs were the same. My gratitude for provision and care remained genuine. But I was tired. The kind of exhaustion that changes your brain.

I wondered if I was ending my perpetual thread of dialogue with God.

Had I lost my way into easy conversation with the Creator? The answer was no. I felt more in tune with him. I was encountering Christ in those trenches. So what was happening?

I wasn't losing touch with God. After years of talking to him and writing more than 20 prayer books and devotionals, I was expanding my view of what it meant to interact with Jesus. I was increasing my ability and willingness to lean into the Spirit and seek hope and leading.

I noticed that my gratitude wasn't saved for a specific time of prayer but was expressed in the moment and *through* the moment. God's responses and my understanding of them were unveiled in the everyday encounters and experiences that were and still are becoming profound and more vivid despite my fatigue. I'm learning to be with Jesus as I live, breathe, sleep, awaken, weep, laugh, connect, hope, fumble, eat, walk . . . . . . and yes, pray.

When we consider our lives to be ongoing interactions with God, we can do as Anne of Green Gables imagines and "feel" the prayer. We can go about our day breathing, living, and being prayer as we offer our lives to God and experience Emmanuel, God with us—when we roll out of bed, roll our eyes at our to-do lists, or roll up our sleeves to prepare for challenges. A deep relationship develops as we willingly become vessels through which God's love can flow upward and outward. From tip of toe to crown of head. From heart's thrum to a dream's hum.

> We can go about our day breathing, living,
> and being prayer as we offer our lives to God.

LIFE as a Prayer

Being tuned in to God's presence leads us to experience prayer as continuous intimacy with him and with our own lives because we're given new perspective and a lens of wonder and wisdom. We are privy to holy nudges that point out what we would've otherwise missed. The splendid color in the blue jay's feather left like a calling card in the garden. The baby in the stroller giggling and reaching toward us in a pseudo high-five gesture, as if to celebrate solidarity in the human adventure. I imagine the Creator leaning in to catch the whisper of our thoughts or the wisp of one of those most-assuredly genius ideas we have just before the alarm clock shocks us into ordinary routine. I anticipate Abba placing a hand on the small of our backs to guide us through terrain we face with our knees knocking. I sigh with gratitude, sensing holy fingers stroking our hair when we're weeping or longing for a tender touch.

We experience life as a prayer when we begin a day willing to look at and respond to people, circumstances, questions, awakenings, and challenges with God's heart. This devotional is a gathering of what I call "slice of life" meditations, along with prompts and offerings that invite you to look at and listen to your life in this new way.

I'm not a fan of spiritual shortcuts, because they usually end up at touristy and trendy emotional places. But you and I want to *live* in prayer, not just visit it. After my season of exhaustion, however, and now during my unfurling back to life, I am grateful for travel companions who guide me with instruction and caring questions, and who create space for me to listen to God. I am thankful for those who, like my gentle-movement class instructors, remind me to seek "ease in the effort" so I can release agenda and experience my pilgrimage more deeply and authentically.

On your journey through these topical devotions, I hope to be this companion for you. I'll settle into the passenger seat, and from that perspective I'll locate the lookouts with breathtaking vistas and spot the roadside stands promising the juiciest spiritual nourishment. You might be tempted to turn up the volume on the radio when I ask what you're thinking or suggest that you slow down; yet you'll be glad you have me along because I always pack snacks like red licorice and Cheetos.

My most important role is to champion your desire to look at life and faith anew. In honor of this role, I offer the acronym LIFE to help us consider the different ways we experience life as prayer:

Longing
Invitation
Forward Motion
Embodiment

When we recognize longing, invitation, forward motion, and embodiment as unique conversation starters with God, we're given new ways to understand our lives as they intertwine with the divine. Let's spend a moment with each of these conversation starters. Consider which ones resonate with you the most right now. Which most draws you toward God? Does one spark a mini-epiphany about a current circumstance?

> When we recognize longing, invitation, forward motion, and embodiment as unique conversation starters with God, we're given new ways to understand our lives as they intertwine with the divine.

Longing

All my longings lie open before you, Lord;
my sighing is not hidden from you.
PSALM 38:9

Longing can be the deep hunger for a missing part of life or self. It can be an ache to become courageous or healed. It can be painful during a season of emptying. It can be a wish for joy and intention. God knows our longings, but it might take us time and a bit of an awakening to know what they are. Yet even while they're hidden from our conscious view, longings often direct or drive our steps, choices, emotions, and endeavors.

My current longing is for a longing. Okay, that might be cheating, but I can't identify my void yet because I'm still working with God to excavate and understand my heart. I've given my longing different names over the past couple of years, but only because I felt pressure to produce a label—sort of the spiritual equivalent of what one blurts out when asked, "What do you want to be when you graduate from college?" So, for now, I experience my longing as a prayer to be drawn into a hope and a vision. I'm able to acknowledge the immediate longings I have in any given moment, from connection to healing to peace. When this is my perspective, my spirit is able to discern what God is doing and what I'm doing to nurture a holy way of being.

> Even while they're hidden from our conscious view,
> longings often direct or drive our steps, choices,
> emotions, and endeavors.

What are your longings today? Do they echo what you've craved since you were ten? Or maybe they are just now being revealed because

11

of a hardship that has stripped away any pretense of having it all or having your act together.

Here are some words of "longing." When these surface in your speech or your prayers, pay attention. Pause with God to identify what he is asking you to notice in your heart.

Hunger	Empty	Want
Wonder	Void	Need
Seek	Crave	Wish
Miss	Ache	Hope

When you walk through the devotions in this book, consider which speak to or shed light on a personal spiritual longing. Let that longing become a prayer, to be filled by God and to have your needs met by his limitless mercy.

Invitation

Listen to your life. See it for the fathomless mystery it
is. In the boredom and pain of it, no less than in the
excitement and gladness: touch, taste, smell your way to
the holy and hidden heart of it, because in the last analysis
all moments are key moments, and life itself is grace.

FREDERICK BUECHNER

This Buechner gem is one of my life quotes. I encourage you to adopt it if you don't have one of your own, especially for our time together. It's a call to attention, a call to witness and experience life through the senses and as grace itself. In every situation, in every moment, you are extended an invitation. Think about it. Arriving at a four-way intersection is an invitation to make a choice. Or that could be considered two invitations: one to make a turn and one to go straight. Spiritual invitations, as prayers, compel us to know ourselves and God better, to seek God's prompting, or to observe our journey with eyes focused and ears tuned in.

If you want to consider where your invitations were over the past week or even the past year, ask yourself when you experienced a nudge to reflect on someone's comment or on the possible consequences of an upcoming decision. When did you feel called to view an issue from another person's perspective? Have you had to change jobs or face downsizing before you were ready? Each of these events is an invitation to experience or examine life differently.

While longings shed light on what might be missing, invitations shed light on where we might be going, who we are, and the condition of our minds, hearts, and souls. An argument can be an invitation to understand why we're so passionate about a subject or why we feel the need to always be right. An emotional response to a friend's offhand comment could be an invitation to become aware of and tend to a wound we guard carefully.

> While longings shed light on what might be missing, invitations shed light on where we might be going, who we are, and the condition of our minds, hearts, and souls.

These invitations-turned-prayers don't all make appearances as heavy decisions or trials. For example, a new friend's upcoming gathering could be your opening to step away from isolation and embrace prayer for finding community. The words on the following list represent situational invitations that can become prayers for discernment and awareness, leading you below surface thoughts and rote responses.

Beginnings	Challenges	Doubts
Decisions	Losses	Questions
Crossroads	Transitions	Choices
Obstacles	Possibilities	Endings

Every invitation to experience God can become a prayer for self-awareness and a deepening sense of God's character, faithfulness, and presence. In your every circumstance, I know God is present and engaged in the invitation it extends to you. As you read through these devotions, you'll be encouraged to reflect, pray, experience stillness and silence, and ask yourself questions you might not have thought about before or perhaps have avoided. Such times of exploration will beckon you to contemplate your life and faith...and will likely reap even more invitations.

Forward Motion

Prayer is an opening of the self so that the Word of God
can break in and make us new. Prayer unmasks. Prayer
converts. Prayer impels. Prayer sustains us on the way.
JOAN D. CHITTISTER

Now we're moving. While the LIFE path doesn't need to be viewed as a progression, you could evaluate where you are in a certain spiritual journey by looking at it as such. For example, if your longing is for purpose, you may have been sensitive to some invitations to explore what that purpose is and how God is preparing you for it. A next step could be to move forward in purpose. Perhaps an opened door, a request, or an accepted challenge is now propelling you onward. Even before "forward motion" becomes our prayer for leading and sustenance, it is our prayer to be freed from a place of stuckness or stubbornness.

Forward motion allows a transition away from old and toward new. It doesn't require quantifiable leaps from A to B. The world likes to count our steps and success-ladder rungs, but I suggest we leave the assessment of value or growth to God. He measures the immeasurable, so who are we to try to gauge the reach of a prayer or the expansion of a heart? "Who has measured the waters in the hollow of his hand, or with the breadth of his hand marked off the heavens? Who has held the dust of the earth in a basket, or weighed the mountains on the scales and the hills in a balance?" (Isaiah 40:12). Answer: God.

I've experienced my most transforming spiritual strides while practicing stillness. Going nowhere, so to speak, is forward motion when prayer is deepened and the soul's receptivity is quickened through devoted attention. Stillness and silence draw us inward to listen to the Holy Spirit away from the buzz of chatter and the ringtones of distraction. The person who ignores the invitations to live out prayer and self-awareness with faithfulness is like the lazy and arrogant rabbit in

15

Aesop's classic fable "The Tortoise and the Hare"—distracted by immediate wants and oblivious to what it takes to move forward in her gifting. Just like the victorious turtle, however, we can rest in knowing that slow progression is nothing to be ridiculed. In spiritual matters, a slow unfolding of truth and self can alter one's course and spiritual condition as poignantly, if not more so, than the bolt-of-lightning revelation.

> Going nowhere, so to speak, *is* forward motion when prayer is deepened and the soul's receptivity is quickened through devoted attention.

Spend some slow and savored time with the words on this next list. Which of these represents your forward motion prayer experience in some way? Or maybe other words have come to your attention as you've started in a new direction.

Journey	Next	Opening
Leading	Toward	Breakthrough
Release	Threshold	Inspiration
Momentum	Freedom	Shift

During our devotional journey, I hope you'll be given insight into how you're moving toward God and his calling for you. Your forward motion might be revealed as a transformed mind, a healed heart, or a voyage of courage on which you embarked with faith and without weighing the cost of vulnerability. Your forward motion might also emerge as the surrendering of a past path as your feet and outlook turn in the direction of what is new and unknown. This is when forward motion becomes a prayer of faith, and sometimes *for* faith in a future.

As the writer and teacher Parker Palmer wrote in *Let Your Life Speak*, "We must trust and use our gifts in ways that fulfill the potentials God gave us. We must take the no of the way that closes and find the guidance it has to offer—and take the yes of the way that opens and respond with the yes of our lives."[1]

Amen.

Embodiment

We should seek not so much to pray
but to become prayer.
SAINT FRANCIS OF ASSISI

This is mighty presumptuous of me, but I believe most any life prayer and experience could be placed within one of these LIFE categories. Although this last one, embodiment, seems a far reach, and maybe even a little pious, for a daily kind of prayer, it isn't. When we look at when we—or anyone—have been the heart of God to the broken, the hands of God to the needy, or the strength of God to the weak, the potentially lofty concept wafts downward to a place of grounding and relevance. Heaven's prayer on earth, you might say.

For clarity and inspiration let's look at one of the most beloved prayers of all time. I'm sure you've read it or heard it before. Even if you've memorized it, pay attention with intention as you read The Prayer of Saint Francis here and pray it anew. Think about how embodiment becomes a life prayer to be wholly God's vessel for love and light.

> Lord, make me an instrument of your peace,
> Where there is hatred, let me sow love;
> Where there is injury, pardon;
> Where there is doubt, faith;
> Where there is despair, hope;
> Where there is darkness, light;
> Where there is sadness, joy;
> O Divine Master,
> Grant that I may not so much seek
> To be consoled as to console;
> To be understood as to understand;

To be loved as to love.
> For it is in giving that we receive;
> It is in pardoning that we are pardoned;
> And it is in dying that we are born to eternal life.

Writer Paula D'Arcy says, "God comes to you disguised as your life." I think when we embody a godly trait or gift, God comes to others disguised as us. Spend some time with these words of Saint Francis and then with this list. Consider how embodiment is a form of a living prayer when you offer these gifts to others:

Service	Truth	Acceptance
Wholeness	Understanding	Ministry
Connection	Presence	Awareness
Authenticity	Unity	Refuge

> When we embody a godly trait or gift, God comes to others disguised as us.

When you "become" courage, you serve others without compromise and with vulnerability. When you embody compassion, you react from a place of empathy and not self-service or judgment. When you become a sanctuary, you extend the shelter of acceptance to friends and strangers alike and nourish them with love. When you show up in the world as a living prayer for healing, you see people's wounds with tender understanding and you give from the wisdom of your wounds to teach, heal, and offer hope.

You've probably heard Gandhi's quote, "Be the change you want to see in the world." Well, you can become the prayer you want to see in the world. You can live out the prayer God wants others to experience.

Your Life. Your Prayer.

I've shaped a journey of devotions about awareness, healing and hope, courage, connection and compassion, joy, faith, sanctuary, and purpose. Accompanying each meditation are LIFE Reflections and a prayer. The questions and ideas—from me, your travel pal—will hopefully help you explore your longings, your invitations, and ways to move forward and embody God's love. The Intentions presented will be especially helpful for the latter two. Let your mind and spirit wander through your response to one or all the LIFE Reflections, or let the inquiries and suggested actions inspire your own questions for meditation. Then the brief prayer can close your time or start a longer talk with God.

As you voyage through days of living prayer, may you experience the affirmation of Isaiah 30:21: "Whether you turn to the right or to the left, your ears will hear a voice behind you, saying, 'This is the way; walk in it.'" Along this way there is transformation, as well as gifts to hold with reverence because they are holy and to hold with gladness because they are meant to be shared. My ultimate hope is for you to make this devotional journey your own as you follow the heartbeat of the prayer that is your life.

This is the way; walk in it.

Life as a Prayer for Awareness

Today Matters

What I do today is important because I am
exchanging a day of my life for it.
HUGH MULLIGAN

Whether you wake up with a record-breaking to-do list or a blank-page kind of day, the next 24 hours are an offering. You are exchanging each and every segment of time, moment of experience, and pursuit of intention for a slice of your lifetime. Today matters. When you feel lifeless, behind, or unsure, you can awaken to the never-before-seen vista of a new day and move forward in it with hope.

Ordinary days become memorable when you turn your act of noticing into prayers of thanksgiving. What sounds of life awakened you this morning? A child asking for pancakes? A farm rooster announcing his day's plans? What shade of blue is the sky at noon? Is it the periwinkle of cornflowers? Or the azure of a tropical reef? Did you walk across your cool, porous driveway barefoot to pick up the morning paper? Or did you slide your feet into cushy, cozy slippers before wandering to the kitchen to make coffee?

The practice of savoring is even more satisfying than the art of making check marks next to your task list. Awareness enriches your spirit and your day's value. As savoring becomes a part of your way of gently moving through your life, you will add life to your life and to the lives of others. Your coworkers and family members will receive the gift of your ability to notice them and their contributions as well as their needs. You will skip over shallow talk and dive into deeper conversations with those you encounter. And your time with God will be sweet, expansive, and unhurried.

Today matters because it is a prayer. It is your offering to give to God and it is the gift you receive from God. Savor every bit of it.

LIFE Reflections

- Ask God to give you a keen awareness of what you're experiencing through sound, sight, and touch. Develop this connection so you more fully experience this life God has given to you.

- Recall a pleasant taste or sound of childhood. Were your senses involved with your understanding of God at the time? Did you taste a grape with wonder and think of your Maker? Did you feel his presence in a very real way?

- When you awaken tomorrow, start the day with the anticipation of goodness and fullness. See how this perspective makes an impact on the unfolding of the next 24 hours.

- Intention: *Today I will pause and take in one particular moment with great attention. I will notice colors, scents, movement, sounds, and my thoughts as ways to connect to God and the gift of this day.*

Prayer

Thank you for this day, God. I will be aware of the treasures and opportunities this sliver of my life holds for me. I've let quite a few days slip by without realizing their significance. Give me eyes and ears and a desire to take in all the goodness of this new day.

A Moment to Breathe

I make the most of all that comes and
the least of all that goes.
SARA TEASDALE

I need just a moment. To catch my breath. To take in wonder. To explore my thoughts. To consider my faith. To reflect on my day. To wait and listen. When I look at my schedule and consider how many moments come and go, many wasted on mindless tasks or rote thoughts, it's no surprise I feel worn-out but have very little to show for it. Moments of silence allow us to listen for the cues and leadings that the whir of our autopilot feature tends to drown out.

What currently keeps you from silence? Is it the busyness of your day, the rhythm of your life, the pulse of your own expectations? Maybe the better question is this: Which came first, the avoidance of silence or the busyness? I believe, for some, the ability to sit with the silence and in silence depends on what they experienced during childhood. Chaos can breed chaos, and calmness can breed calmness. However, if we experienced an extreme of either of those, we might crave the other out of a desire to protect or comfort ourselves. While some of us are more naturally inclined to crave solitude, I believe we're all created to experience those moments of silence and of seeking. This is when we can feel and know God's presence.

Still moments before God allow us to find a trusted place to stand and welcome what the day has to offer. We are less likely to cling to the burdens of yesterday or clench our fingers around today in anticipation of tomorrow's possible concerns. Honor this day. Celebrate its unfolding as you celebrate your own awakening.

LIFE Reflections

- Consider what keeps you from practicing moments of silence. Prepare a place or a time that allows for a bit of refuge.

- What does the clamor of your routine sound like? Traffic in motion? Coworkers in conference? The cries of little ones? The ring of a cell phone? Wait for these sounds to settle. The voice of God is beneath them.

- Find a comfy place to sit, set a timer for five minutes, and choose a brief personal prayer or simple verse to hold in your mind. Run your thoughts over it like a river runs over rocks. See which words sway the direction of the flow. Which words break through the surface of the current formed by the momentum of repetition?

- Intention: *I will notice when I am restless or anxious so I can tend to my mind, body, and spirit with a moment of stillness to be with God.*

Prayer

God, grant me a heart, mind, and spirit open to all that today offers. Help me make the most of what comes my way and make the least of what goes. Show me the way to stillness when I am restless. Reveal to me the ideas you want me to dwell on.

An Awakened Faith

They have eyes to see but do not see and
ears to hear but do not hear.
EZEKIEL 12:2

When I get run-down or overly stressed, a haze covers my thoughts and I react in slow motion. I lack control of my body. My arms and legs don't feel like my own. A friend will point to a big bruise and ask what happened, and I shrug my foggy "I dunno" shrug. More times than not, the bruise was formed when I walked into the rocking chair or hit my hand against the buffet in the dining room, both of which have been in the same locations for years.

Unfortunately, these times of weariness and emotional survival can cause more than a bruised knee. These times of internal processing and disconnect from my outer world cause me to be careless with my words, comments, and attitude. I stop watching for and listening for God's direction. I don't have the energy to care about what unfolds each day or who around me has needs. The social and spiritual filters I should use to determine when something I'm about to say is helpful or hurtful are defective. My careless responses and remarks can bruise the feelings of those in my path. I don't listen patiently to my spouse. I become blunt instead of tender with friends. And my social graces all but disappear when I have to mix and mingle or just make it through the 15-items-or-fewer line.

When we are spiritually worn-out or hard-hearted, we can also experience a time of wandering aimlessly, in a haze. We become careless with our hearts and our sense of truth, and we tend to run into obstacles more frequently. It is as important to find ways to stay spiritually alert as it is to stay mentally alert. The way to health in both categories can be similar. Pray more, rest more. Get fed spiritually, eat healthily. Make time for fellowship, take time for friendships. Break away for spiritual reflection, give yourself a break. This will lead to your awakening.

Care more about this life you're walking through; it is both physical and spiritual, and nothing less.

LIFE Reflections

- How have your spiritual and physical lives shown signs of weariness?

- What has caused the most heart bruises in your life? The careless words of others? Intentional harm inflicted upon you? Did you tend to those injuries at the time they were caused? Or have you avoided recognizing those crimson marks because the pain is too intense? Spiritual awareness might reveal a few of these hidden wounds. Isn't it time to care for and nurture all of you?

- How can you use this time of refreshment to restore clarity and hope? Why do you want to be "awake" in your faith and life?

- Intention: *I will start each day with a focused prayer, asking for eyes to see and ears to hear. I want to experience my day with God's senses.*

Prayer

Remove this haze from my life, God. I want to be fully aware of each day and each opportunity to grow in my understanding of faith and hope. You provide rest for this weary child of yours. Thank you for prodding me and guiding me so I am awake and engaged.

It's Getting Crowded

If one does not know to which port one is sailing,
no wind is favorable.
SENECA

"Did I turn off the oven? Are my tags about to expire? Will our tree fall over with the next big wind? Let's see, if the mortgage check went through before the utilities check, I might be in trouble. Did I drink the last of the milk? I wonder how long this road construction can possibly last! The price of stamps went up again…"

These can be my thoughts in the span of a split second. Whether I'm driving to a meeting, standing in line at the grocery store, or walking down the hall after a late-evening trek to the bathroom, thoughts like these storm through the sorely ineffective barricades in my mind and take over my conscious and subconscious life. They leave me unfocused, frazzled, and longing for direction.

It's getting too crowded in here…in my mind and heart. I'm filled and overflowing, but not with the reflections my life and spirit crave. I want to spend moments fully aware of mercy's tenderness, of God's leading, of gratitude's buoyancy. But it takes concerted effort to quiet the crowd of daily surface details and musings to get to the depths of God-thoughts.

Turning our attention to peace and stillness with intention gives us a chance to be still in the chaos of overactive thought-storms. If we allow time to ponder our direction, our hearts, and those deeper thoughts that rumble below the chatter of the mind, we'll be in tune with our lives and the direction in which God is leading us. This is our chance to do just that, to make the effort toward intimacy with God. So many concerns and ideas are worth contemplation. Wait for the crowding to die down and clear some space to explore purpose, redemption, and the joy of being alive in this moment.

LIFE Reflections

- Identify and list which recurring thoughts keep you up at night or interfere with your concentration during the day. Spend a few moments praying over these specific concerns.

- Was there ever a time when you more readily explored questions of God, faith, and wonder? What can you do now to recapture that spiritual level of contemplation?

- What image gives you peace? Spend five minutes looking at a painting, photo, or view out a particular window that stills your rambling thoughts. Talk to God about a specific longing, hope, or need. Spend another five minutes listening with your heart. Hold this space as a harbor for holy engagement with God.

- Intention: *When my mind becomes scattered today, I will fix my thoughts and heart on one particular prayer. I will pay attention to the peace that comes rather than anticipate a certain outcome.*

Prayer

Lead me to your feet, Jesus. I want to sit and listen as you speak truth into my life. Keep me from crowding out those times when a song of praise rises up in my spirit or a prayer drifts from my heart to my tongue. These times will honor you.

Dawdle

I used to be an expert dawdler. As a kid I loved to get lost in music and books; they transported and filled me. I'm sure arguments exist against cultivating a mind that so readily goes to the interior, but this was the beginning of my quest for creativity and invention.

Sadly, the world of adulthood has shifted me toward productivity, deadlines, tasks, and a preference for getting things done. This way of life doesn't nourish my soul. I've lost the ability to quickly and gladly settle into a vacation day or a book. Worries override my ability to imagine my day differently. I want to see my life with fresh eyes and a creative mind each morning.

Learn to dawdle with me. Whether or not you were ever good at it, give it a try. Sitting in silence can work. Lighting a candle is a start. Gazing at the moon for 15 minutes after the rest of the household is asleep is fabulous. Heading to your backyard with a glass of lemonade and a book on a summer afternoon is right on track. Lying in a hammock in the shade of a tree while your mind drifts to how you'd like to grow your garden next year is perfect. When you catch yourself trying to rush by slower people at the grocery store or along a river path, hold back. Breathe in. Walk to match their pace. They might be expert dawdlers, and you could learn a lot from them.

LIFE Reflections

- Have you been able to dawdle as an adult? Were you able to as a child? Choose to spend time with a friend who helps you let go of your inner critic so you can embark on a few hours of guilt-free dawdling.

- What frees you? A palette of vibrant colors? An afternoon of no responsibility? A warm, lazy summer's day? A blank page in a sketch book? Discover what sparks your sense of creativity and frees your spirit.

- What keeps you from savoring life? Spend time exploring the obstacles so you can overcome them and fill your life with more whimsy and wonder.

- Intention: *Even if I have to schedule it, I will take time for dreaming, napping, staring at flowers, drawing scribbles, skipping stones, or whatever strikes my fancy.*

Prayer

God, help me to still my spirit. Guide me toward the deeper waters of stillness and reflection. Show me how to make the most of an afternoon by "wasting" it with nothing planned. May I use the gift of dawdling to praise you, serve you, and discover more about life's riches.

What Springs Up

Inside myself is a place where I live all alone, and
that's where I renew my springs that never dry up.
PEARL BUCK

Awareness isn't only about seeing and doing what is in front of us. Awareness is also about seeing what we ignore. Spiritual awareness leads us to uncover the intangibles that seek our time and affection. Those mental distractions we shoo away may be exactly what we are meant to pay attention to. If we're sitting at a table with our bills splayed out and our checkbook open, and our mind wanders to how we'd like to go on a mission trip to Brazil, a dream has just attempted to capture our attention. Dreams, goals, life questions, and prayers emerge when we least expect them.

The multitasking nature many of us have adopted has its benefits, but what falls by the wayside are those brief encounters of understanding that surface and require more thought and consideration. We're too busy cleaning out email inboxes, sending texts, and answering phones, and the spiritual leading gets squelched. Exchanging efficiency for spiritual deficiency is not a good trade.

Practicing awareness ultimately requires us to give credence to our hopes and musings when they spring up. Sit with them. Give them space in your life to be considered. Our heart longings don't come to us as whispers because they are unimportant; they emerge as whispers because they deserve our undivided, rapt, lean-on-the-edge-of-our-seats attention.

LIFE Reflections

- Spend less time shooing away dreams and more time musing over them.

- When was the last time you listened to your dreams? How did God use those dreams to deepen your connection to your purpose or to him?

- Can you think of an idea you squelch on a regular basis? Give it space. What about it scares you, excites you, and challenges you?

- Intention: *Today I will actively listen for my heart to speak up, and I will be prepared to take notes. I will pay attention to find out if a prayer of longing or invitation is emerging in my life.*

Prayer

I want to be centered and not scattered. Teach me the wisdom of silence. When my spirit resists silence and I fill my time with activities and my ears with voices, music, media, and dialogue, lead me to the quiet whispers of my soul and of your will.

Start a Trend of Truth

When a woman tells the truth, she is creating
the possibility for more truth around her.
ADRIENNE RICH

You are a creator. You are an artist forming your life's work under the instruction of the Master. What you put out into the world is your creation. When you work hard to establish a comfortable, caring atmosphere in your home, you are creating a sanctuary. If you raise children to love others and to celebrate God, you are inspiring faith. When you speak kindness and peace into the lives of people who face pain and turmoil, you're inventing a life of compassion.

What you do today can set the trend for those around you. I love the fruit of the Spirit presented in Galatians 5:22-23. Look at them afresh as the materials God gives you to create a life's work that is honorable and holy. Love allows you to honor all of God's children. Joy celebrates life, and peace leads you back to God's presence. Patience waits for God's leading. Kindness reaches out without discrimination. Goodness inspires greatness in others, and faithfulness does not waver in the face of insecurity. Gentleness eases the soul, and self-control reflects discipline and commitment.

As you look at your life as a creation, consider what other "materials" God has given you to shape a life. Then consider how your background, personality, and experiences give you a unique perspective that comes through in all you do. What quality might be considered your artist's signature? Kindness? Discernment? Playfulness?

Create a life that draws out your best and stirs a heart of faith in others.

LIFE Reflections

- What are you creating? What are three positives you can express about what you have created?

- Return your thoughts to the fruit of the Spirit daily. Find ways to express each of them through your actions, your intentions, and your efforts. Let go of behaviors that don't reflect the fruit of the Spirit. Pare them away.

- Are you someone who holds back from showing others what you create? Consider how you might take a small step forward with courage to share more of your life. Pray for opportunities to be real with others.

- Intention: *I will find ways to create goodness. I will become more willing to trust others and share more of my life.*

Prayer

I've rarely considered my life to be an act of creation. I want to view each day as an intentional offering to you and to others rather than as an unremarkable passing of another 24 hours. Help me become whole, balanced, consistent, and true in all I do and say and profess. Where I am weak, help me glean strength through my trials and questions. Where I am false, help me dig deeper until I uncover the root of my insecurity and exchange it for your truth.

What a Life Produces

It is within my power either to serve God or not to serve him.
Serving him, I add to my own good and the good of the whole
world. Not serving him, I forfeit my own good and deprive
the world of that good, which was in my power to create.

LEO TOLSTOY

You can tell much about a life by what it produces, by what comes
forth into the world from that life's effort and existence. The works
of our hands and hearts are often compared to harvests in the Bible. I
consider the produce of our lives to be a matter of faith and faith alone.
What pours forth from our efforts, love, and decisions reflects what's
going on in our hearts. When we produce crops of complaints, arguments, destructive language and actions, self-hatred, and anger, our
hearts are distant from God's leading and we've stopped tapping into
his unconditional love as our source for life.

Athenagoras, a philosopher and Christian apologist in the latter
part of the second century, described the Holy Spirit as an effluence
of God. That struck me as a lovely and profound explanation. The
Holy Spirit flows out of God. It makes sense to me that the outpouring of God is the Spirit. They are one, and they are separate. Ah, the
confounding mystery of the Mystery. But we're not going there; we're
going to your heart. If God is your center, goodness and joy are the
effluence of your soul, your speech, your thoughts, and your intentions. Do love and abundance flow from your faith? What else does
your faith produce? Gladness, passion for dreams, deep empathy for
those in pain, a hunger for justice, and an abiding love for God and his
children? (All his children, not just those who look like you or share
your opinions?)

During your time of reflection, consider what's flowing from your life. Do you emanate a peace that is of God? Instead of trying to have influence with power, money, or emotional leverage, won't we offer the world much more healing and joy if we desire to be an effluence of faith?

LIFE Reflections

- What flows from your life now? What would you like to be the effluence of your daily living?

- The joy of a harvest is that there is abundance to share. Give of whatever God produces in your life. Choose three specific ways to do this.

- Sit with the Holy Spirit today. Ask to embody a characteristic of your faith so you can express the outpouring of the Spirit in the lives of others.

- Intention: *I will be mindful and prayerful today so the harvest of my efforts and actions are goodness, joy, peace, and kindness.*

Prayer

Show me how to love with your love, God. Show me how to be joyful and generous with the bounty of faith you give to me daily. May I never hold back a portion of your goodness so others may receive these offerings freely.

Expect More

Don't live down to expectations. Go out there
and do something remarkable.
WENDY WASSERSTEIN

Responsibilities can be overwhelming, but let's face it, many obligations and privileges come with being part of a family—or part of the human race, for that matter. I have friends who are simultaneously managing the needs of their children and those of their elderly parents. Some things we sign on for; some are part of the life cycle.

Turn your attention to those aspects of your life that have a lot of weight and influence. Do you ever feel as though you're living for someone else? That you've taken on someone else's expectations for your life? Expectations are different from responsibilities. When expectations shape your motivation for the day, they can turn your life inside out as you try to please someone other than God and live a life that isn't true to your purpose or calling.

If the expectations placed on you by others don't resonate as true for you or your happiness, start declaring your own. Life is way too short to be dictated by guilt and guilt-based decisions. I don't mean you should pack your bag and head for the hills (you still have responsibilities). Instead, search your heart, seek God's leading, and find the direction that is your very own. Wouldn't it be great to live for God as he intended? Go do something remarkable! What are you waiting for?

LIFE Reflections

- If others have low expectations of you, step away from those limits and those deceptions.

- If you bought into the idea that you're not worthy of goodness, then you have settled for a false, low expectation. Spend time daily in prayer, asking to receive a deeply felt sense of your identity as God's child and cherished creation.

- Discover how freeing life can be when grace replaces guilt. Teach this transforming perspective to others through your actions, responses, and willingness to listen with acceptance and reverence when they share their feelings and experiences.

- Intention: *No more listening to guilt and expectations in stereo. I'll turn up the tune of grace and hum along.*

Prayer

Guilt. I know it is not of you, God. It never has been. I used to rely on conviction that did come from you, and that gently guided me in the right direction, toward big love and sweet mercy. But then I started listening to guilt and the expectations of others. I should've known that being bullied into righteousness was not your will. Reveal to me the leading of the Spirit and allow me to hear and follow only your voice.

Just Visiting

Teach us to number our days and recognize how few
they are; help us to spend them as we should.
PSALM 90:12 TLB

A few years ago I had the wonderful opportunity to spend time in both my birth town and the city where I lived after college. One is small-town America and the other is an expanse of urban blocks. During my nostalgic visits, the simplest things triggered a deep sense of joy. A field of corn set against a darkened summer-storm sky. A girls' softball game and the aroma of hot dogs coming from the snack shack. The brick building where I had my first career position. The boarded-up windows of a deli-and-pie shop that used to be my regular breakfast stop. The pine plank-floored bedroom in my first childhood home. Each piece of my past was enjoyable real estate to walk through, but it also felt good to just be visiting. Not because I couldn't see myself in these places again, but because we should never take up residence in days gone by.

You might not walk along the town square of your youth, but maybe you frequently return to a past incident, a time of suffering or affliction, or even a happy time you've been unsuccessfully trying to recapture. We have much to learn from the earlier legs of our journeys. Why do we have the humor we do? Why do we say our *R*s or *O*s with a bit of an accent? It's good to notice what we have adopted permanently into our personalities or sense of priority.

But we are never meant to live in our pasts. God lives with you in the present. This morning he will greet you with leading and love. This afternoon Christ will plant a seed of hope in your situation of concern. This evening, in the quiet, he will ease your concerns and remind you of your many blessings. Today God is shaping you for your life right now. Don't be tempted to live anywhere else.

LIFE Reflections

- Where do you reside during your restless days or sleepless nights? Are you lost in a past circumstance? Can you instead live today as God leads?

- Think on what you are grateful to have brought along from your past…good habits, sensibilities, faith, and so on.

- What is happening in your life that grounds you in the present moment with gratitude and joy?

- Intention: *I will take up residence in my life as it is now so I can celebrate what happens today and have hope in tomorrow.*

Prayer

God, usher me into the present when I linger over the past too often or for too long. When I revisit my hurts, remind me of my healing. When I start to wish for times gone by to resurface, remind me that today is where you and I connect and where you are guiding my steps.

Life as a Prayer for Healing and Hope

How to Rebuild a Life

Our real blessings often appear to us in the
shape of pains, losses, and disappointments.
JOSEPH ADDISON

half-joke with friends that I'm planning for my personal breakdown.
That's the result of my controlling personality trying to orchestrate
how to fall apart in a responsible manner. Yes, I am possibly delusional.
I know a breakdown isn't controlled. But I do believe they can be pur-
poseful. Breakdowns are not pretty to the world, yet they can be beautiful. They aren't the way we want to change our lives, but they can be
a way to freedom. The old needs to fall away for a reason. The new life
requires a beginning built with God's purpose and hope. When God is
rebuilding your life and your faith, he will:

- Break down the walls built during past pain to build up
  the power of forgiveness.

- Break down the coldness of religiosity to build up the intimacy of personal faith.

- Break down the stereotype of success to build up the truth
  of abundant living.

- Break down the need for control to build up readiness for
  divine guidance.

- Break down the expectations built up to build up the
  promises of God.

Our transformation is taking place when we watch life as we've
known it crumble around the edges and sink into the faulty foundation of anger, pain, regret, and emptiness. It might look like loss, but

45

it's the image of gaining abundance. It might feel like starting over, but it's really about moving forward. Faith wasn't built in a day. Okay, I borrowed part of that line, but it's still true. What lasts isn't built overnight. We can receive saving grace in an instant, but faith is ongoing and evolving because it's a relationship with a living God. Those times of tearing down will lead to the rebuilding and restoration of your faith and your life. Don't try to salvage the ruins. Spend time with the Architect and celebrate the new plans he's unfolding.

LIFE Reflections

- The word "blessing" is thrown around a lot. What does it mean to you?

- Can you view a recent loss or struggle as a blessing? Do you see how your deconstruction is leading to the rebuilding of faith and hope?

- The new thing God is creating in your life will lead you forward. Trust in that. Let this season become one of a forward-motion prayer for renewal.

- Intention: *I will stop building walls so I can see the life being rebuilt by God's compassion and peace.*

Prayer

God, as much as I want to rest in the blessings of this trial, I'm not there yet. Today, may I just rest in your shelter? I look forward to the restoration I know will come. Your faithfulness in the past builds up my faith today, and I am grateful.

Intentional Waiting

If we could for a moment see the cosmic implications
of our waiting with and for God, we would be
astonished at the glory of "ordinary" things in our
lives, and the significance of other people.

ISABEL ANDERS

If we were in control, we would collect all those minutes "lost" while stopped at traffic lights, on hold on the phone, and waiting in lines, then deposit them back into our life accounts. But, thankfully, that isn't an option. If we pay attention, these occasions of worldly waiting are a training ground for spiritual waiting. Maybe there is no differentiating between the two. All forms of waiting become a spiritual practice because they require us to recognize that we are not in control—one of the hardest lessons we'll ever face.

But when we wait with and for God, we have even more important lessons to embrace. We discover beauty in our wounds. We learn to accept gracious help from others rather than take pride in our independence. During our wait for physical healing, we learn more about our need for spiritual healing. As we long for transformation, God grants us a vision of hope to carry us and those around us. When waiting feels less than divine, we have the opportunity to see how complete reliance on God is an extraordinary gift. And when we long for God's leading, but end up waiting and wondering if the wait is in vain, the One who is in control makes a deposit of faith in our life accounts.

LIFE Reflections

- See waiting as an opportunity to grow spiritually. What gifts have you received during times of waiting?

- How has independence kept you from full reliance on God? Do you wear your personal strength as a badge of honor? Let God be the one you honor. Be willing to make a mistake or show weakness. These vulnerabilities will become your invitations to a deeper, more substantial faith.

- What are you waiting on God for right now? Pray specifically for this during your waiting moments throughout the week.

- Intention: *I'll spend time deliberately looking for the glory in the ordinary.*

Prayer

I have allowed my distorted sense of priority to dictate how I view waiting. I get frustrated when I'm asked to slow down or to hold back from rushing forth with my plan and agenda. God, pace me. Show me the rhythm of life that leads to greater understanding of you. Teach me the spiritual blessing of waiting.

Growing a Problem

Some people are making such thorough plans for
rainy days that they aren't enjoying today's sunshine.
WILLIAM FEATHER

With a handful of snow and a fresh trail of more white ahead, I can easily turn a wimpy cluster of water and air into a rather large, dense mass. I spent a childhood indulging in this metamorphic process of turning a small lump into a life-sized snowperson. Maybe this is why I am so diligent and talented at rolling small problems around in fresh patches of thought. Each roll adds weight and mass, giving the problem a much more substantial position in my mind. When my conditions are just right for negativity—a bad experience, an anxious heart, naysayers around me, or a rough self-image day—that hypothetical what-if is no longer minuscule but looks life-sized and rather daunting. It's so big, in fact, that it can cast a shadow on today's decisions, attitudes, and perspectives.

Are you rolling a mass of what-ifs around in your mind with vigor and determination? Isn't it amazing how it can feel productive to grow our problems? Over the years, I've realized if I let in some sunshine, these growing blobs begin to disappear. Positive thoughts, the prayers of others, encouraging readings, enjoyable activities, and friendships warm up my thoughts and start to shift the internal storm toward a brighter day.

The next time you roll the same old problems around a new day's worth of clean thoughts, step into the warmth of good thinking and positive actions. It is so much better to see your problems melt down and avoid a mental meltdown of your own.

LIFE Reflections

- How have you snowballed a possible problem into a certain obstacle?

- Why do you think you bring old problems or worries back into each day's new thoughts? Where did you learn to do this? Do you worry about what would fill your mind if you let go of these old patterns?

- Tomorrow, give yourself the "day off" from the practice of building up concerns. If a problem gains some momentum in your thoughts, imagine it melting. Turn your thoughts to the warmth of God's peace and provision.

- Intention: *When old worries pop into my mind today, I will say, "Today is for the light of new thoughts," and I will let the things of old melt away.*

Prayer

I'm so tired of these anxieties and hypothetical problems, God. I know I waste the provision of each day on these useless worries. Help me to let go of them and to see them for what they are—obstacles I have created. I want to see how my life will be filled with goodness when I let go of fear.

Today Is for Living

Trust the past to God's mercy, the present to God's
love, and the future to God's providence.
AUGUSTINE

If I were to ask you to describe your past failings and regrets, would your response be so vivid, detailed, and clear that the truth would be known, that these failings and regrets are not at all in your past but are very much in your present? Do you keep such things alive by giving them time and meditation, both of which are gifts you could be giving to God instead?

It's time to discard past mistakes and let yesterday do the job it was made for. Yesterday is our wise teacher when we glean its many lessons. Yesterday is our testimony when we can share about our transformation through faith and God's love. Yesterday is our reminder that God can lead us through loss and error and pride and pain. But yesterday should never be our substitution for today.

If your regrets are alive and kicking, it's because you're fueling them with current thoughts and nurturing them with the oxygen and space of your present. Do you need help carrying those regrets to the foot of the cross? Are you ready to leave them for dead? Because the power of the resurrection doesn't exist so you can resurrect your mistakes and tend to them; it exists so you can live abundantly in the present and have hope for a future. God's mercy has covered those difficulties and mistakes so you can be alive in the moment. So you can be used for greater purposes than being a life-support machine for your past. You decide each and every morning what you are going to give your presence and passions over to today—the unchangeable past or the abundant and transforming present.

LIFE Reflections

- Which regrets do you nurture and keep alive? Are you prepared to give them up for something better?

- Old wounds can reopen time after time. They can start to feel like an acceptable normal when they are instead an unfortunate obstacle to wholeness. Let them truly heal so they are a source of wisdom and not pain.

- If you have a friendship or relationship with someone who lingers in yesterday's turmoil rather than today's promise, show them God's mercy. Accompany them with the language of grace.

- Intention: *Today I will make sure my regrets are not being nourished by my actions and thoughts. I'll give energy and effort only to today's hope.*

Prayer

I'm so glad to have moved on in my life. I don't want my past failings to become my focus today. I have so much more to experience in this moment and in the future because of you. Redirect my thoughts and my sense of direction. Lead me away from yesterday. It has done its job.

The Fullness of a Good Life

Be a good steward of your gifts. Protect your time.
Feed your inner life. Avoid too much noise. Read
good books, have good sentences in your ears.
Be by yourself as often as you can. Walk. Take
the phone off the hook. Work regular hours.

JANE KENYON, FROM *A HUNDRED WHITE DAFFODILS*

We can be filled with many things and in many ways. We can stuff our faces, our souls, and our hunger places without giving much thought to what we are reaching for to fill a void that makes itself known. Several times a week I catch myself scanning a movie channel's guide, the inside of a kitchen cupboard, a search engine's offerings, or a clothing rack to see what seems like the best, temporary filler. In the middle of the act, I know I'm not seeking a way to be truly sated, that I'm willingly choosing something that will ultimately leave an aftertaste of regret. And I do it anyway.

It takes awareness and a level of care to figure out what we are truly hungering for and then to search out what will provide nourishment. The writer Jane Kenyon provides a great list in today's epigraph. Those joys that feed our spiritual cells are not always considered "holy," yet they can become holy when they are a part of our practice of living life as a prayer. When we choose to fill our minds, ears, mouths, thoughts, and hours with what is good rather than what simply happens to be available, we reap the rewards of a fed inner life. The restlessness abates and we can be still before God. In time, most of us will realize that our deepest want—the hunger beneath the agitated, distracted searches for satisfaction—is for communicating and communing with God.

The next time you feel empty and on the prowl for comfort, consider what you might offer to God. Are you willing to give him your searching heart and your roaming mind so he can, in the stillness, fill you with his love?

LIFE Reflections

- When a gnawing lack makes itself known, pay attention to your first response. The better you know yourself and your moves, the better you will be able to step back and recognize what spiritual food you need.

- In which areas of your life do you overindulge? In which areas of your life do you starve your heart, body, or soul? Look after these areas with tender care. Seek God's balance so neither gluttony nor frugality destroys your spirit.

- Create a list of words, people, places, ideas, objects, and dreams that bring you joy. Meditate on this list and keep adding to it. Say these aloud sometimes when you are alone. The sound of blessings spoken is surprisingly powerful and healing.

- Intention: *When I'm scrambling to fill an emptiness, I will pause and ask God to help me understand what it is I am truly hungering for. I will make a choice that soothes the soul.*

Prayer

God, lead me to your nourishment. Help me to see these times of want and agitation as opportunities to understand myself and you better. When I'm tempted to ignore the tug of the Spirit to stop and notice my life and my longings, remind me that you are right there with me and are eager to point me toward the fullness of a good life.

Where Does It Hurt?

Let God's promises shine on your problems.
CORRIE TEN BOOM

I bet we both have faced hardships and surprises and times of need, and so you and I have come through a lot. When we've gone through extreme difficulty and our lives seem fragmented by the cuts of sorrow, healing comes to us in different ways. Our ideas of what healing will look like and what it will free us to do once our damage has been repaired are so limited that we are likely to miss out on the restoration we receive.

Our healing might be taking place in a different area than the one so blatantly marked by our pain. If you've prayed for restoration in a relationship, your healing might come in the form of a new perspective about that relationship. You might need to labor through the healing and then be willing to see that relationship anew on the other side of your efforts. "Fix me" or "Fix this" might be our heart's cry, but "one remedy suits all" is not usually how God's healing manifests in our circumstances. God is personal in his interaction with us and in how he soothes, comforts, and leads his children. Our pleas represent where we are emotionally, often coming at our crisis points. And his promises are true and far-reaching in our lives.

God sees our lives from beginning to end. From joy to sorrow to joy again. From need to abundance. His balm reaches the places within us we might not know are broken. So our desire for physical healing might be met with physical healing, or it might be met with spiritual healing. Observe with open eyes and an open heart so you can recognize the healing of an emotional wound that has long needed the balm of God's peace.

LIFE Reflections

- Where do you hurt? Ask God to shine light on the source of those hurts.

- Change your prayer from "Fix this" to "Be with me in this, Lord." Rest in God's presence.

- Have you given thanks for past times of healing? Acknowledge God's continuous work in your life. It helps you to recognize your healing in all circumstances.

- Intention: *I will share the joy of my healing with someone. I will make known the goodness of redemption.*

Prayer

Comfort me, God. I want to have my pain soothed and my wounds healed. Prepare my heart to see and accept the way healing is manifested in my life. Thank you for the balm of your peace and love. Let today be the threshold I walk through on my way to days strengthened in hope.

Gold for Sorrow

Be truly glad. There is wonderful joy ahead, even
though you must endure many trials for a little while.
These trials will show that your faith is genuine. It is
being tested as fire tests and purifies gold—though
your faith is far more precious than mere gold.

1 Peter 1:6-7 nlt

Someone once told me that, in some cases of extreme grief, a gold compound has been given to patients as part of homeopathic treatment. I found that fascinating. I realize the doctor didn't say, "Swallow two class rings and call me in the morning." Nevertheless, I still found the concept of a precious metal used as medicine to be captivating and poetic. Like gold, our lives can be put through fires. The flames that touch and refine our faith are those of suffering and grief.

During our most personal and overwhelming trials, we have the gift of faith. We can lean into our faith and find rest. We can step under the covering of our faith in God for refuge. As the verse above illuminates, our faith is more precious than gold, especially for our healing. Our hope in God's peace and purpose carries us during seasons of sorrow.

When someone you care about is facing the shock of grief, it's through faith that you can be a source of strength and comfort. You can be a companion for their journey by being prayerful, tender, and generous. Your presence might encourage them to enter God's presence, where they'll experience mercy far surpassing human compassion.

As sojourners of faith, we have something else that leads us to hope and healing: "The laws of the Lord are true; each one is fair. They are more desirable than gold, even the finest gold" (Psalm 19:9-10 nlt). Try as we might, we cannot fully comprehend the mysteries of life and death, but we can cherish the pursuit of God's truth. We can desire, even in our sorrow, the beauty of a wound healed and the sacredness of a faith refined.

LIFE Reflections

- How has your faith been refined through the fire of trials or disappointments? What part of your life do you hold on to tightly because you fear the fires of heartache or loss? Entrust God with that area and turn your longing for control into a longing for faith.

- Exchange your sorrow for God's healing. You'll get a great return on it!

- Do others in your life know the value of God's mercy? Extend compassion so they feel the hope of healing. Help them to feel seen, heard, and held with love.

- Intention: *I will release my overprotective hold on my life so I can hold up God's healing as a priceless gift.*

Prayer

God, your comfort sustains me. You hold me up when I want to sink into grief. The refuge you provide is hard for me to explain to others, and yet I hold on to it with absolute faith. You are with me in joy and in sorrow. Nothing is of greater value than your love.

Birds of a Feather

Two people are better off than one, for they can
help each other succeed. If one person falls,
the other can reach out and help.
ECCLESIASTES 4:9-10 NLT

When the change of season brought sunnier weather, my friend enjoyed the opportunity to sit outside and be entertained by the sweet birds that emerged simultaneously with the colorful new blossoms that bordered her yard. The feathered, lively tourists congregated daily around her pond and drank, ate, and bathed with contentment. After several days she noticed these birds had a built-in system for support and protection. One bird always stood "guard" while its peers took care of life's necessities.

We face many changes of season in our lives. Whether the change is brought on by ageing, loss, transition, or opportunity, we rely on our flocks to help us along. Maybe someone drives you to the doctor's office, a neighbor watches your kids on short notice, or a friend delivers dinner when life is just plain overwhelming. The family we are born into as well as the one we create present a way for us to experience God's support and protection.

I'm grateful for the times a friend has offered to help me before I even had a chance to ask. When people are perceptive enough to discern what we need and when we need it, they become vessels for God's provision. These moments, in turn, inspire us to be aware of what needs we might be able to ease in our near and dear circles.

We all long for and deserve friends who stand with us or for us and who have our backs while we take care of life's necessities. And our lives are richer each time we can be that friend for one of our own when they face their challenge of change—big or small.

LIFE Reflections

- What season are you facing? What seasons are your friends and family members facing? Spend time thinking about these seasons. What do you discover about the needs that come with these times? Let this awareness be your invitation to pray about those needs and the ways you can become a source of help to others.

- Do you entrust your times of hardship or change to your flock? What situation do you need help with right now?

- Are you reluctant to accept help that comes even from friends, let alone strangers? Consider how they are moving forward in obedience or faithfulness when they offer assistance and concern. Ask yourself if that is something you really want to be blocking or negating. It is humbling to receive certain kindnesses. Let your pride fall so someone else can rise up in compassion.

- Intention: *I'll accept help today. And I will humbly accept the prayers and support of those God brings into my life.*

Prayer

Give me the strength I need to make it through this transition. I have hope for tomorrow even as I struggle with today. You have blessed me with friends and family who seek the best for me. I pray for the willingness to share my burdens with this support network, and that I will come to you with my every need.

I Wish I Knew

When you get into a tight place and everything goes
against you, till it seems as though you could not
hang on a minute longer, never give up then, for that
is just the place and time that the tide will turn.
HARRIET BEECHER STOWE

I wish I knew what kept you up late, staring at the dark while chasing shadows in your mind. You're dealing with stresses others aren't even aware of, and yet you keep a brave face until you're out of public viewing and in the solitude of nightfall. You're being brave so the people you're caring for don't realize their needs are overwhelming you. You're being brave because you haven't seen an alternative to being stoic and solid and always available to others.

I wish I knew which past hurt echoes through your soul today. You don't put it out there in conversation, even with close friends, because you think it would surprise and baffle people to know the poignant pain that burdens you most isn't the accident, illness, loss, or other "defining moment" they assume is the cause. I'm not surprised. I understand that seemingly small hurts are the easiest ones to carry around in your heart's pocket and revisit every free moment.

I wish I knew what worry makes your heart skip a beat each time you step outside your comfort zone. How the offhand comments of another leave your mouth dry and your palms sweaty. I imagine you have days that tick-tock along as though they are years because your energy is spent pretending you're fine and your hope is spent on survival instead of healing.

I wish you knew how much I pray to the One who does know every bit about you and who holds you in a great, protective embrace. Maybe this would bring you comfort. Maybe this would encourage you to allow that embrace to save you along this journey.

LIFE Reflections

- Who in your life doesn't know the love of God is a personal, transforming love? Commit to pray for them each day this week.

- Consider the way you hide your own loneliness or pain. Most people you meet have those same hurts. Extend grace to everyone you encounter today.

- You can't always know what someone is going through, but God does. Trust his leading. When people pop into your mind or make an appearance in one of your dreams, take that as an invitation to pray for them. Becoming aware of others and lifting them up to God will expand your capacity to love.

- Intention: *When people lash out or pull back, I will not take it personally, but I will cover them in prayer. I will cover myself in prayer.*

Prayer

Lord, I pray for those who have pain so deep that they barely make it through the day. Give me a heart in line with yours so I can offer the words and actions people need. You've been my healing refuge during times of pain. Remind me how it felt to be cared for. Give me an active empathy that is far-reaching and never discriminating.

Life as a Prayer for Courage

Imagine the Possibilities

Nourish beginnings, let us nourish beginnings.
Not all things are blest, but the seeds of all
things are blest. The blessing is in the seed.

MURIEL RUKEYSER

When you're around possibility thinkers, do you get nervous? Do their grand visions make you tighten your grip on your perceived, limited reality? Or maybe you're one of those dreamers who make other people's palms sweat. I find myself to be somewhere in between. My mind is often in the puffy clouds of dreams and ideas, but my legs feel as though they are stuck in cement when it's time to make a move toward those possibilities. Not always, but this happens often enough that I question when I will truly live with faith and courage.

In the movie *You've Got Mail*, there's a sweet moment when Meg Ryan's character sadly announces that she's going to close her beloved children's bookstore. She views shutting the doors a final time as a failure, a terribly wrong detour away from her long-served dream. But her wise mentor is eager to share a bold truth as she pours her distressed friend a cup of tea: Closing the store is the brave thing to do. It is? Meg's character seems shocked. It is! It is opening up to the possibility that a new life exists. Oh, how this speaks to me. Isn't it a prayer of hope and wonder when we say good-bye to a situation, form of security, relationship, or way of doing things, and dare to rest in God for what comes next?

Bravery is rarely intertwined with a moment of success. It often exists in its purest form in the instant of uncertainty when we turn our feet in a new direction and are trembling with self-doubt. That's when we reach for God with more determination and dependence, and the beginnings of a new purpose takes hold in our hearts.

LIFE Reflections

- Consider whether you are a dreamer with wings or a dreamer with legs tethered to the ground. Was there a time when you soared toward passions and beginnings with more ease?

- What are you holding to tightly that you need to let go of, close, dismantle, or give away?

- As you spend time in prayer and stillness, what new possibility is being presented? What brave thing might God be calling you to live out now as a forward-motion prayer?

- Intention: *When I next experience a great resistance to an area of change, I will pay attention to whether it's the exact area God wants me to bravely move toward.*

Prayer

Creator of dreams and beginnings, give me the courage to release what no longer serves my purpose. Show me the way through the difficulty of an ending so I might experience the joy of trusting you for a new way of being.

Facing Our Cure

Our tendency is to run away from the painful realities
or to try to change them as soon as possible....Cure
without care makes us preoccupied with quick changes,
impatient and unwilling to share each other's burden.

HENRI NOUWEN

Don't let me see it. I'll focus on the places I feel whole, complete. Most of us, at one time or another, have believed that looking away from our hurt would make the situation better. Maybe right now you and I are both hoping for a painful situation to be changed immediately or even taken away. Or we think if we don't see it and it heals up—or more likely, it becomes buried beneath layers of busyness—then maybe we can press on with life as though the hurt never happened.

We can feign wholeness, right?

But this choice overrides the response to lift up a soul-felt prayer for help and healing. The gift of a wound is there for us only when we look at it. The light of healing is visible through the cracks, the breaks, the holes in us. Jesus's wounds are the place where we witness the light of resurrection. We can watch for this power to radiate from our most vulnerable places.

It takes courage to look at your wounds and fresh scars. And it takes faith to believe they will lead to hope and to opportunities to care for others with empathy forged by fully experiencing the most painful experiences.

You will need guts without the promise of glory to present yourself as flawed, open, gaping. But don't turn away. See what shimmers through the places of pain. You won't want to miss the beauty of your mending.

LIFE Reflections

- Have you been reluctant to look at a past hurt? Pray for God to be with you as you turn your eyes to that open wound or pink scar. His mercy will keep you safe.

- Watch for the ways your hurts have been or are being transformed by God into the holiest layers of your being.

- Your wounds shape you into a new creation. Can you look at them with some appreciation? Welcome the gifts they might offer, such as a greater capacity for compassion and understanding and a deeper sense of gratitude.

- Intention: *I will look on my hurts with tenderness and treat them with appreciation. They are a part of me and I am loved wholly by God.*

Prayer

God, I have shown you my hurts, but I've been afraid to look at them. I worry they will define me or prove I'm beyond repair. When I trust in the light of your healing, I can begin to see the hope of resurrection in my own life. And I can believe that my wounds can serve others.

Escape Routes

Backup plans are nice, even practical and healthy. I consider myself extremely mature and wise when I think through the best- and worst-case scenarios of a situation and chart out another path to success. But what is going on when we jump from strategically mapping out a backup plan to cleverly plotting a back-out plan?

You might be someone who follows through with every commitment and never thinks of finding the nearest exit when facing obligations, events, and activities that make you uncomfortable. But I bring this up because I personally like to have an escape route when I face a new situation or attend a gathering. Sometimes I've scheduled another appointment after an event so I have a forced cutoff point. I often rejoice when an activity is canceled, because when I get out of something I feel a surge of excitement. It's like a snow day in grade school. I anticipate the free time and the possibilities of how I'll fill it.

As rebellious and whimsical as they feel initially, however, our back-out plans eventually black out our dates of availability for what God has planned for us. If we dictate exactly how our lives should unfold, we are never open to God's plan for us. If we spend our energy searching for an "out," we will never be in God's will. But when we step into each new situation with an open mind and an open heart, we get the most out of God's plan.

Let's put our energy toward mapping a way out of mindsets and habits that keep our lives restricted and controlled. It will be the greatest escape of all.

LIFE Reflections

- Do you ever hope events will be canceled or that you can bow out of a commitment? Consider if you are overextending yourself or if you're worried about being vulnerable, attached to community, or called forward in a purpose that feels scary right now.

- How have you tried to escape responsibilities or relationships? Why did you have that impulse? Do past hurts affect your present-day attempts to live a whole life?

- Entering a new situation is easier when you release control of the outcome. I know that's hard to do, but it works. Try it with something you're facing this week.

- Intention: *I will spend time praying for and mapping out a way to leave behind fear and move forward in faith.*

Prayer

God, you are the only backup and safety net I need. Help me to resist placing my expectations on the people and moments in my life. I want to greet each possibility with an open mind and a trusting heart. Show me the way to go. When I hesitate to go forward in the direction of commitment or community, release me from my worries. My assurance and strength are in you.

Needing a Good Try

You must do the thing you think you cannot do.
ELEANOR ROOSEVELT

What is the thing you think you cannot do? Let me throw some possibilities out here for you. Maybe you struggle to be yourself with a specific person. Speak in front of a group. Pursue a big geographical or professional move. Write a novel. Start a business. What is that thing? You know what it is. It might be covered up by thoughts of what you have done recently or even in the past that you're sure have bought you some time and wiggle room before anyone (yourself included) starts asking, "Why haven't you ever done…?" But I am here right now asking you this question. Don't worry, I have my own confessions. In fact, most of the opening examples relate to my list of things I say I cannot do, for one reason or another!

It's time for us to have a "good try." I don't mean to try harder, work harder, or strive and struggle more. No, not that kind of "try." I mean for us to try more often than not. Say yes to something that makes the hair on the back of our necks stand at attention. If the word "yes" gets caught in your throat from years of avoidance, then come up with your own yes-phrase. *Sure thing. You betcha. Wouldn't have it any other way.* Or use an oldie but goodie that might at least make you laugh: *Okey-dokey.* Sure, we're tricking ourselves, uttering what amounts to still saying the Y word, but sometimes we need to do this to push ourselves out of old, worn habits we should've retired years ago.

Make a go of it. Give it a chance. Give yourself a chance. Give God the chance to show up and show strength through you. Isn't that worth an okey-dokey?

LIFE Reflections

- Who or what situation convinced you that you couldn't do this thing? Was it you? When did you start telling yourself this? After one time of tripping or even falling flat on your face? Whatever that moment, look at it now with self-compassion. Look at it from God's view. What did you learn from it?

- How did God show up for you in your hurt or disgrace? Maybe that moment can be cast in a new light that frees you to pray for challenging opportunities and mean it.

- Face your life with gusto, faith, and the courage to fail, and you will become sensitive to the prodding to move forward in purpose. Layers of self-protection feel great initially, but they begin to separate us from the sensations of our skin and soul. A life that is a prayer emerges when we strip away all that comes between us and God's touch and voice.

- Intention: *I will look for a way to have a good try today. I will take one step toward whatever was formerly known as the thing I cannot do.*

Prayer

Okay. Alrighty. Yep, yep. I give my nod to you, God. You and I both know what the thing is I say I cannot do. It's been my thing for many years, but I'm ready to look at it with excitement rather than fear. This thing will be my way to lean on you more. Let my life be a prayer of acceptance today. Amen!

Willing to Dream

Every great dream begins with a dreamer. Always
remember, you have within you the strength, the patience,
and the passion to reach for the stars to change the world.
HARRIET TUBMAN

What do you want to change about your world? When your heart breaks because there's so much pain and suffering, have you forgotten that you are here to make a difference? I shake my head at the problems around me. I take these concerns to God in prayer. But I know that because I am God's child, I am to do more than notice those who hurt. When I see injustice and judgment where only grace could possibly heal, I can be that giver of grace.

Ask God to shape your dreams and set a longing in your spirit to participate in the healing the world needs. It's a big request, and many of us are afraid to state it for the record. What if we don't know how to right a wrong or mend a heart wound? What if our capacity to love the unlovable is too limited? What if this step disrupts the life to which we have grown accustomed? If these doubts expressed as questions hold you back from asking God to give you his dreams for your life, then ask him for his heart first. It is tender and willing and open. Ask God for his eyes. They see others clearly, they envision the big picture, and they witness the hurting world.

God doesn't tire of answering questions about hopes and desires to find a path or vocation that serves others. Tug on his sleeve. Ask for clarification and direction. And seek his presence as you allow your dreams to form in the real-life dimensions. Changing the world isn't something you do alone.

LIFE Reflections

- Will you replace your dream with God's dream for you?

- How have you felt directed to change your corner of the world? Have you ignored a dream from earlier in your life because it seemed beyond your ability? Bring it back out and dust it off. See if it still holds a sense of calling for you. It's never too late to believe in God's ability over your own.

- Be a healer and a dreamer. Live in God's truth, speak words of kindness, and reach out with acts of compassion.

- Intention: *I will let myself dream without listing the reasons why the hopes on my heart are not possible. God is the reason they are possible.*

Prayer

I want to be a big dreamer who is willing to leap into a life so much bigger, deeper, greater, and more significant than I could ever imagine. This abundant life is the one you have mapped out for me. You direct my steps and prompt my heart. Give me the courage to move forward toward this gift.

A Brave Grace

Courage is fear that has said its prayers.
DOROTHY BERNARD

Life requires courageous steps, big and small. Sometimes just getting out of bed is an act of bravery. Following God's leading when it's outside of our expectations or plans is an act of courage. Trusting God's forgiveness when we perceive ourselves as unworthy is an act of courage. And that kind of courage is ours only when we depend on God through and despite our fears. Such trust in God's power becomes a part of our character when we face head-on a conflict, a need, or an average day with prayer. When we can look at our lives—including our weaknesses—as an offering, as a sacrifice to God, then we are acting with fierce faith.

I don't feel courageous when I'm sinking. I don't feel brave when I tremble with self-doubt. But during these times I do become more willing to release my determination to survive in my own power. If I fall, I want to fall into God's resilient grace. I want to "say grace" and know what it means in the grit of the daily grind.

"Saying grace" seems an old-fashioned term for prayer. Rarely do you hear this particular phrase at a dining table where pizza is served and those gathering around are 15 minutes late to soccer practice or eager to get back to their phones. Yet saying grace is a way to introduce our side of grace—giving thanks. Bring the act of giving thanks back into your life and the lives of your family members. It will lead them to greater faith. It will lead them to gratitude. It will lead them to courage.

LIFE Reflections

- Why do you feel unworthy? Sometimes the thing, person, or event that initially caused us to feel unworthy is not even in our present life. We've just been afraid to believe in something better.

- In what ways do you exhibit strength and truth?

- Spend time giving thanks for your recent joys, your latest problems, and those past happenings that gave root to bitterness. These all are meant to lead you to God. What could give you more gratitude than that?

- Intention: *I'll embrace courage as a God-given character trait, and I will give thanks.*

Prayer

I've spent a lot of time dwelling on my fears. Even though I know you and your peace, I turn back to the way of fear. Lead me through these times. When simple worries morph into a foundation of fear, I will return to the courage I have in you. I need not tremble. I need not avoid living. Thank you for every circumstance that turns my thoughts back to you and my heart toward you.

Benediction of Gratitude

We need to remind each other that the cup of sorrow
is also the cup of joy, that precisely what causes us
sadness can become the fertile ground for gladness.
HENRI NOUWEN

Today is the day the Lord has made; let us rejoice and be glad in it."
Some mornings my husband calls this out from the encouragement found in Psalm 118:24. If I haven't hit my snooze alarm thrice, I call out "Amen" in response. And I mean it. Awe and pride both rise up when I hear this morning blessing, because I know he's choosing to sip from the cup of gratitude. And he is sharing that cup with me. Who am I to refuse? I haven't faced the hardships he has in the past few years. I have supported him, I have stood by him, I have prayed for him, but I have not faced the physical trial that has been his journey. The gifts of compassion, prayer, and generosity I have known during this trial lead me to the cup. When I witness my husband's willingness to celebrate a day, not because it's easy but because it is a gift, then I'm compelled to lift the cup to my lips.

If we reject gratitude until we experience a perfect day or our lives become uncomplicated bliss-fests, then we will not partake of it. Perhaps ever. We don't produce gratitude. Success doesn't produce gratitude. Gratitude comes from God. Do you realize your present reason for perseverance is also a reason to be grateful? Can you face a future of unknowns, standing on some hard-to-face knowns, and still rejoice in the possibility of hope and goodness? If so, then you have come to the cup of gratitude. Drink. Today is the day the Lord has made; let us rejoice and be glad in it. Can I hear an "Amen"?

LIFE Reflections

- What have you let keep you from sipping from the cup of gratitude?

- Will you give your heartache to God so something meaningful can be made from your pain?

- Find ways to open up your life to receive blessing and express thankfulness. Consider focused times of prayer or journaling. Create lists of what you are grateful for this week, this season.

- Intention: *I will see gratitude not as a reflection of my circumstances, but as a response to my God.*

Prayer

I've wanted my trials to be taken from me, and yet they lead me to the cup of gratitude. I am ready to be filled and renewed. May I turn my heart toward you with appreciation that flows no matter my circumstances. When the cup is bitter, I can still sip with thanksgiving. Your presence makes it sweet over time.

Freed During the Resistance

His gifts are free for the taking, but I cannot
take these gifts if my hands are already full
of my own weapons of self-protection.
KATHERINE WALDEN

In my adult life, I've been part of a resistance. At some point I started to resist the abundant, complete life God was presenting. I said no thanks to travel when staying home sounded more comfortable. I shook my head no when the intimidating challenge of trying something new arose without advance notice. I held up my hands to ward off a life trial, and then spent the entire span of that trial resisting the lessons it was teaching.

But I can't tell you why. It's funny how you think you know yourself well, but then discover you've been doing things behind your own back. Life-changing things. Like saying no to the life nudged your way over and over again. As I look back at all these paths not taken, these refusals, these excuses that cloud my perception even today, I'm pretty sure I've done more resisting than embracing.

If you can look back on your life and witness a picket line of complaints, excuses, rants, and refusals, then you might be a part of your own resistance. I have wisdom for both of us:

You can't hug something when your arms are folded across your chest in defiance. That sounds a lot like a quip attributed to a spunky Southern grandmother, but whatever way you hear it, read it, or take it in is fine by me—as long as you embrace its truth and stop resisting the lovely life being offered to you.

LIFE Reflections

- What do you resist the most in your life? Help, love, tenderness, challenge, sadness, or growth? Take time to prayerfully figure out why you say no to good things.

- Resistance comes from a place of self-protection. See if you can view each decision and opportunity as a way to peace. Welcome these issues into your life so you can see how God's peace surpasses our limited understanding of what is good for us and what can harm us.

- Take a glance back at the past six months. What lovely people, opportunities, or adventures has God presented to you but you were not ready to receive? Consider your life as a prayer for courage as you open the door to these gifts now.

- Intention: *I will say yes to more things this week to break up my routine and the limitations I've set on my life. I'll accept the good, the bad, the doubts, and the duty tied to each opportunity.*

Prayer

Just this week I said no to something I was supposed to say yes to without fear and resistance. God, grant me the seed of hope I need to unfold my arms and unfold a life of wonder.

Courage After the Healing

Birds sing after a storm; why shouldn't people feel
as free to delight in whatever remains to them?

ROSE FITZGERALD KENNEDY

I've had the opportunity to lift up prayers for healing on behalf of someone I love. And together we've witnessed and experienced healing. We approach God with hearts full of gratitude for the gifts of well-being, hope, and recovery. But life doesn't look the way we thought it would. So how do we carry the hope of healing into this new experience?

Just as we don't always recognize the way healing has manifested in our bodies, relationships, hearts, and beliefs, we don't always recognize the post-healing life as the one we are intended to live out with conviction and peace. Because we're looking for a return to the life we once had, we don't recognize the revised version of life we are given instead. Healing does not drag us back to the time before the hardship; it moves us forward in knowledge, peace, and intimacy with God.

Are you experiencing life post-healing? Does it look different or fall short of the vision you had for life after the pain? This season, too, may come with limitations and difficulties. Pressing on in this new version of your experience is still part of your healing. As tough as it can be, it's nevertheless a gift to see your days with new eyes, to walk with strength and appreciation toward different goals, and to modify your expectations and begin living abundantly in your purpose rather than in your preconceived notions.

Loss and suffering and times of paralyzing disbelief change us from within. We don't come out on the other side as the same people who went into our trials. You are now living as a person who has been touched by transformation, renewal, and grace. Embrace the newness of healing.

LIFE Reflections

- Are you on the other side of a trial and still trying to make sense of how your life is now? How is it different? How is it the same?

- Can you let go of how you thought life would be after healing? God knows your life's big picture while you only experience a peephole version of it. Step forward into this healing.

- Does disbelief creep into your thoughts and prayers? Allow grace to cover your doubt.

- Intention: *I won't watch for the human version of perfection, but I will seek the healing that comes from the Perfecter of my faith.*

Prayer

I'm trusting your healing, God. I welcome it and will walk forward in it. Remove those expectations I've placed on what life will be or should be. Open my heart to the wonder of your hope for me personally.

Birthing Pains

Each day you must say to yourself,
"Today I am going to begin."
JEAN PIERRE DE CAUSSADE

This is the year. My friends feel this could be the year we do more than merely contemplate and mull over our ideas. This could be the time we put our ideas out into the world and see what comes of them. The life of an idea begins at conception, but the power and influence of that idea begin when we send out the birth announcements.

Unfortunately, many of us prolong the gestation period. Procrastinators, late bloomers, or those who believe they're not original, creative, or smart are the women with the longest gestations. Sorry to say this, but we're the elephants of the idea world. But I also have some good news for us. We, the plotters and the planners, are often the ones who give birth to the biggest, strongest, most fascinating ideas. We just have to be willing to go through the labor pains.

Why is putting forth our ideas so painful, anyway? Why are we afraid for our ideas to see the light of day? Personally, sometimes I'm afraid the world will take one look at my idea and call it ugly…unworthy…puny. I believe somewhere along the way we have forgotten that our ideas are part of God's creative purpose for our lives.

Follow through with the birthing of those ideas that grow within. You've been carrying them and protecting them. Now it's time to push them forth. Don't worry about what others will say about them. Just love them. Nurture them. See them as a wonderful, exciting extension of you, your heart, and the One who made you.

LIFE Reflections

- Are you gestating like an elephant? Isn't it time to birth that idea?

- Ideas aren't intended to be born fully grown. They are supposed to be out in the world for a while before they're mobile or speak to others. You'll be able to nurture them as they grow.

- What holds you back from pushing your dreams forward?

- Intention: *This is the year, the week—the day, even—when I will give life to a new idea or to one I've held close to my heart for far too long.*

Prayer

God, you give me dreams big and small. Guide me to follow your leading as I strive toward them. Connect me with others who will also nurture the dreams you want to see unfold in my life. May I strive to bring forth things of goodness and worth in your eyes.

Moving On

It takes some of us a lifetime to learn that Christ,
our Good Shepherd, knows exactly what He is
doing with us. He understands us perfectly.

PHILLIP KELLER

When my third-grade teacher announced to my Iowa grade-school class that I was moving to Oregon, she pulled down a large United States map with its vast masses of blue and green. She first pointed to Iowa, nestled comfortably in the middle, and then to a location so far on the left that she had to stretch her arm to reach it. It seemed about as far from my childhood spot in the universe as Mars. It was a visual that reinforced what I already felt emotionally. I was leaving the center of the world. Who wants to say good-bye to the life they have known and start over?

As an adult I have several friends who had to make big moves. A couple of them faced significant geographic jumps (I resisted unveiling a vinyl map and pointing out just how far they were going), and one had to make major shifts in career pursuits. They all faced the big task and trial of sifting through their belongings. From shredding old bills and filing photos to wrapping vases in bubble wrap, they prepared to pare down life so they could be flexible enough to embark on a journey.

These times of moving on are difficult—physically, emotionally, and spiritually. We grow roots in community, in familiarity, and in security. These are all good and vital to our survival, but times of uprooting and transition are also part of survival and of goodness. When you can embrace a change in time zone rather than linger in your comfort zone, you will discover God's provision. When you can press on during a change in direction, you will discover God's faithfulness. When you are able to make God the center of your world instead of yourself, you will make strides toward a plan and purpose…even when you have to stretch your life to reach it.

LIFE Reflections

- Are you having to stretch your life so far right now that it hurts spiritually, emotionally, and physically? Have you ever had to?

- Do you trust God as the Shepherd of your life?

- Can you view changes in direction, location, or life patterns as a faith adventure? Each kind of change is a chance to grow in faith and discover the depths to which you can depend on God.

- Intention: *I will view change as an opportunity to live more intentionally and to trust God more faithfully.*

Prayer

Lord, I'm giving you my days, my needs, my choices, and my trust. Faith can be a bit scary, but I'm in this for good. I will walk in your way, and I will reach out to embrace the adventure of a lifetime.

Life as a Prayer
for Connection
and Compassion

Learning a New Language

If we use no ceremony toward others,
we shall be treated without any.
WILLIAM HAZLITT

When you become fluent in a language, you not only learn vocabulary words and verb conjugations; you also study conversational customs and rhythm. When talking to a stranger or a business proprietor, Spanish speakers initiate conversation by making a personal connection. They ask how the other person is doing, and then they wait for a response. These inquiries are not only pleasantries, but also extensions of respect, courtesy, and kindness. They are invitations to connect.

When I think of how task focused I have become in my interactions, I find my behavior a bit shameful. My mind usually skips past pleasantries and goes straight to an objective. I have many excuses. I feel scattered or forgetful much of the time, and I don't want to lose my train of thought (have you ever tried to stop a moving train?). Also, I'm a prime representative of a culture that's self-focused, in a hurry, and disconnected. My false sense of urgency overrides the need to connect with others at a personal, heart level. The problem is…I'm missing out on a lot of the dialogue of life.

To engage in true dialogue with others requires that we first offer up a bit of ourselves and then invite them to join the conversation. That can often be a scary, vulnerable, or time-consuming choice, but it's the most direct way to speak heart-to-heart with others. When we stop talking at them and start sharing with them, we achieve a deeper connection.

If you desire to become fluent in the language of faith, invite people to dialogue, and then stay long enough to learn a little something. Become an interpreter of the complex heart language.

LIFE Reflections

- Start a conversation with the intention of learning more about or encouraging the other person.

- The language of faith takes practice. Not so it becomes rote, but so it becomes authentic. Seek to be authentic in the words you choose and the way you respond to the comments of others. This will lead to deeper dialogue. What word seems to represent your spiritual journey right now?

- Embody your adjectives, such as "kind," "caring," "attentive," "open," "inviting," or "authentic."

- Intention: *I'll make the effort to live out my verbs—"love," "listen," "hear," "accept," "respond," "believe," "pray."*

Prayer

God, let me speak to those I encounter with respect and consideration. Give me sensitivity to hear the needs of others, and give me patience to relate to and respond to what they aren't saying. Steady my mind when it wants to leap ahead and anticipate what to say next or what tidbit of wisdom I can interject into a conversation. Remind me to listen to the person you place in front of me and to trust your leading to become an open, welcoming receiver of another person's story, experience, heart-need, or prayer.

Potluck Faith

Who is greater, the one who is at the table or the
one who serves? Is it not the one who is at the
table? But I am among you as one who serves.
LUKE 22:27

I've had a strange, recurring idea lately. It involves clearing away our living room furniture to make room for a cluster of tables. It requires the act of inviting people from different subgroups in my life to enter our home and share a meal or two or three. This vision is especially crazy because I don't cook. It's a bit uncomfortable because, as a personal rule of thumb, I prefer solitary experiences over group ones. And it's risky because I don't know who would show up and what the event would be like.

What do you do with random "potluck" ideas that tug at your heart? Are you someone who finds change difficult, even when it seems to be God's leading? Numerous times I've resisted the convictions of the heart. With my 20/20 hindsight, I see how those were missed opportunities to grow and to inspire others to grow.

Is God leading you toward connection with others in new ways? How would following this call expand your life, enrich it, complicate it, rescue it? When we say yes to opening up our hearts, we often don't know what we'll get, but we do know of a few certainties: We will be scared and restless and even frustrated about changing the way we do things. But we will discover new things about ourselves, others, and God's nature. This is the very reason to join the mismatched gathering of hungry folks at God's table. You will fill up on strength, mercy, and wisdom…and you will be asked to share this feast with others.

LIFE Reflections

- How are you called to serve others or to create community? What keeps you from following this leading? Follow through with small ways to be more inclusive and to share your life.

- What are some of the most absurd ideas you wish you had followed through on in the past?

- What opportunity is rising up in your life right now that you want to embrace?

- Intention: *Today I will light a candle and enter God's presence. I will sit at his table, eager to be filled with his love and compassion for others.*

Prayer

God, lead my heart toward the uncomfortable ways of growth and the remarkable ways of hospitality. Rid me of my expectations and my desire to control the outcome so that I can overflow with your love. May I see every person as your child.

Pre-Ramble

A loving silence often has far more power to heal and
to connect than the most well-intentioned words.
RACHEL NAOMI REMEN

Words get in the way of communicating compassion. We get in
the way of communicating God's heart for others. Have you
ever tried to express your sorrow, only to have a friend interrupt and
introduce her struggle and sadness? I've done it to others, and I've had
it done to me. I think it's a natural response. It probably comes from
a desire to connect with the other person's need. That's the forgiving
viewpoint. After all, what says "I understand" better than explaining
our own encounter with a similar problem, plight, or loss? And doesn't
it say we understand more than others if we also talk about a cousin's
journey through the same challenge, how we were by her side, even
when it cost us time and energy that we'll never get back?

Nope.

Compassion doesn't have to be communicated along with your
bio, résumé, family tree, or pain credentials. Others don't always need
hard proof that you can empathize. They need gentle proof, the kind
that comes with nods, hugs, and prayers. Sometimes your testimony
will give great relief and comfort to other people. But before you begin
to speak, take time to listen. Listen to a wounded friend's words and
body language. Don't rush people toward a resolution for their situation because there might not be one...not today. And don't force your
own tidy answers onto others' difficult circumstances; you'll stifle their
willingness to share their doubts and deepest needs.

Most importantly, when they struggle to find the right words,
stand with them in silence. When you feel uncomfortable, that's the

beginning of true empathy. Often it's in the silence that a heart awakens to God's healing.

LIFE Reflections

- How uncomfortable are you with the silence of another? Is it your pain or your friend's pain that you rush to cover with words?

- Consider several ways to show compassion to another that involves only actions, thoughts, or prayers—and not words.

- Start spending a few minutes each day in silence. Be intentional about this commitment so you can become more comfortable with silence and so being silent is a more natural way for you to listen to your own heart and to God's leading.

- Intention: *I'll learn the languages of sorrow and of comfort and become proficient at listening to both.*

Prayer

When I am the person in need of the healing silence of compassion and friendship, I first seek you and your presence. You offer a balm that eases my deepest worry, my sharpest pain. I look for this care from others, and sometimes it's there. But sometimes it cannot be found. Give me a discerning heart when I'm around anyone who weeps or who longs to weep.

Mercy, Mercy Me

The wisdom that is from above is first pure, then
peaceable, gentle, willing to yield, full of mercy
and good fruits, without partiality and without
hypocrisy. Now the fruit of righteousness is
sown in peace by those who make peace.

JAMES 3:17-18 NKJV

For such a gentle word, the act of mercy is courageous and transforming when it is bestowed and experienced. True mercy is given
by one who has power over the one who needs forgiveness. A judge
grants mercy to an offender of the law. God is merciful toward his
broken children. In daily life we have opportunities to offer mercy to
others, and such an opportunity often involves allowing a "gotcha"
moment to pass on by. Mercy very well might require that we swallow
our own pride.

Rather than lord our power or influence over a friend or loved one,
we can express compassion. If you're struggling to remember a time
when you felt as though you had any power at all, you might be looking for the wrong kind of power. We do have strength. We are placed
in situations when we can and should forgive another. If a visiting child
breaks a family heirloom, you have an opportunity for mercy. When a
waitress spills hot coffee onto your hand instead of pouring it into your
mug, you can show mercy. If a driver edges into your lane because he
made a last-minute decision to exit the freeway, you are gifted with a
mercy moment. The day a friend returns a borrowed, dry-clean-only
sweater now shrunken and tiny, try mercy on for size.

I didn't say mercy was easy. I said it was gentle, courageous, and
transforming. Share your new understanding of mercy when you're

placed in the position of judge, teacher, or parent. Your mercy will generate the gift of peace for yourself and others.

LIFE Reflections

- When have you shown great mercy? When have you not shown compassion for another and regretted it later?
- Train your heart and mind on God's love so mercy becomes your nature.
- If you enjoy or desire having power over someone else at work or at home, step back and give that situation to God in prayer. Chances are you'll need a pride adjustment.
- Intention: *I'll extend grace and mercy to everyone I meet today.*

Prayer

My fuse seems so short lately. God, grant me a heart that expresses real compassion. I know the truest, deepest, most transforming compassion because of your grace. Help me to pass it on, especially when my pride wants me to correct, limit, or judge another.

Give Freely

I have found that among its other benefits,
giving liberates the soul of the giver.

MAYA ANGELOU

Vivid scenes of famine and poverty in distant areas can move us
to tears and compel us to send money to a place we've never vis-
ited and pray for people we've never met. These are good impulses.
But many of us struggle with compassion in our own circles, our own
towns, and our community centers. The close proximity of poverty and
pain can make us uncomfortable, even as our hearts ache for the need
we see in our immediate vicinities. Spreading love and our resources
to the ends of the earth is a good use of our time and priorities, but
we cannot do that and still neglect sharing God's love with those closest to us.

Being a physical representative of Christ's love for another is a powerful act. When we first reach out to others and touch their shoulders
and look them in the eyes and express compassion, we will understand
the importance of this personal, intimate connection with God's children. What does it look like to be Christ's hands? We are his hands and
his heart when we're serving a meal at a homeless shelter, reading mail
to an elderly neighbor, giving someone money without conditions,
cooking for a friend who's ill, holding hands with a person in the hos-
pital, or listening to the needs and life story of a stranger.

This isn't an easy or comfortable step for a lot of us. It requires a
vulnerability that can feel awkward and even painful. Reaching out to
another requires us to reach beyond our norm. So we can pray, and
we can start by first noticing the hearts and aches of the people in our
own homes. Then those of our neighbors. Then we can expand our

awareness to the people we cross paths with on our way to work or as we run errands. Giving and loving freely actually frees us and others to change the world with the unconditional love of Christ.

LIFE Reflections

- When you ask to see the needs and hurts of others, you will. Prepare to be prayerful and to draw from God's compassion.

- Have you wept for the heartache of another? Don't hold back from empathy. It connects you to the brokenness of others and then back to your own brokenness. Ultimately, it leads you right back to God's heart.

- Consider ways to be the hands of Christ. Preaching the gospel is for some; living the gospel is for all of us.

- Intention: *I won't turn away from those who are hurting. Instead I will reach out and make a connection.*

Prayer

God, where are those needs? I'm ready to see them and respond to them. Even the people closest to me are good at hiding their pain and ignoring their need. Show me how to be vulnerable so they are invited to do the same in my presence and in yours.

Potluck Faith in Action

A longing fulfilled is sweet to the soul.

PROVERBS 13:19

That vision I had about hosting a potluck? Well, it materialized. And, of course, it had nothing to do with my planning. It was all God's doing. I'm sure he knew if I was ever going to put that idea in motion, it would take many months and maybe even some counseling. As much as I wanted to open up my home and life to others, I also knew I'd have to give up control and my need for everything to be perfect. What took place was so much better because it was out of my control. All I had to do was say yes to the opportunity God carved out for me.

And wouldn't ya know it, this all came about on Christmas Day.

Snow and ice made the driving conditions unsafe for my husband and me to travel to be with family, and on Christmas Eve we made our final decision to remain at home. Then we called a few friends who were also staying in town and invited them to Christmas dinner. I was full of gratitude for our home, for our friends, and for God's profound presence in our lives during the past year. All day I was aware that, on a small, manageable scale, the potluck vision had materialized. It wasn't the big chaotic event I first envisioned (and been scared by). It was a time of fellowship that unfolded simply and graciously. I know it was just the beginning of how that dream will take shape in my life.

Over time, God forms the desires of our hearts and also orchestrates how they will appear. It might take us a moment to recognize a longing fulfilled, a hope met, or a prayer answered, but these realized dreams are appearing all the time. In the light of God's goodness and hope, you will see your realized dreams for what they are…a gathering of gifts for your faith journey.

LIFE Reflections

- How has God unfolded a hope that has been on your heart? Take time to reflect on these happenings. They have not materialized by accident. They are purposed, significant gifts.

- Do you have desires of the heart? Sometimes we operate on autopilot for so long that we forget to dream and nurture those hopes. Give yourself time to consider what God is placing on your heart.

- Is God encouraging you to play a role in fulfilling another person's dream? Consider this a privilege. Seek peace and humility so your inclination toward busyness or insecurity doesn't become an obstacle.

- Intention: *I will hold on to a hope and a vision God has given to me, and I will move toward them with gratitude.*

Prayer

Give me a heart for the desires and plans you have for me, God. May I greet each day as another 24 hours in which I can delight in those desires.

Believing in Ourselves and Others

There are different kinds of gifts, but the same Spirit distributes them. There are different kinds of service, but the same Lord. There are different kinds of working, but in all of them and in everyone it is the same God at work.

1 CORINTHIANS 12:4-6

Have you ever needed support desperately, but because you wouldn't trust others to step up, you didn't even ask them for help? Or have you requested help even though you didn't expect anyone to follow through, but then been pleasantly surprised by care and assistance?

Have faith in others. Watch for their goodness and their good works. Every day will bring instances that remind you of the faithfulness of the heart formed by God and for God. Don't underestimate the courage or the compassion that abides in your neighbor, the man looking for work, the woman at the checkout counter.

Have you been the recipient of someone's faith? I'm not always a gracious receiver of other people's confidence. I'm sure they're wrong if they think I can do something I believe I can't do. Talk about jaded! Sometimes this response comes from humility, but more often than not it's from a place of fear. Either I'm afraid of letting them down or I'm afraid that maybe, just maybe, the life God is calling me to is bigger than the one I'm ready to live. Now that I recognize this internal tension, when people suggest obstacles for me to overcome or ventures to pursue, I try to squelch my initial excuses or list of reasons why they're crazy wrong about my strengths. I resist asking for a recall on their votes of confidence. And I imagine resting in divine strength and the belief that God is nudging me to explore a different gift, talent, or area of service.

Presume the best about people, including yourself, and you'll discover the best of humanity. If we commit to this perspective, we'll understand why and how "God so loved the world," and why and how he is calling us to do the same.

LIFE Reflections

- When have you been surprised by an individual's response to a need or to a community's outpouring of kindness?

- How do you respond to needs you see around you? Are you depending on God to have other people step up while you hold back out of fear or a lack of motivation? Take a life inventory and see if God and others have been nudging you toward a challenge, an area of gifting, or a way of connection.

- Allow yourself to be amazed by compassion. Ask for help. Believe in the faithfulness of others.

- Intention: *I'll believe in myself and the people I encounter today. I'll embrace potential more than impossibility.*

Prayer

I'm not always quick to believe in people. I want them to prove themselves. Guide my heart away from fear so I can open my eyes to the faithfulness of others. I want to see you in the goodness around me in friends and strangers alike.

Life as a Prayer for Joy and Creativity

Unguarded

When we were children, we used to think that
when we were grown-up we would no longer
be vulnerable. But to grow up is to accept
vulnerability…To be alive is to be vulnerable.

MADELEINE L'ENGLE, *WALKING ON WATER*

Do you take joy in the smallest of things? Or have you become a bit cynical, always prepared to brace yourself for the worst-case scenario or for someone's judgment? Many of us have become guarded. Cautious. Doubting. Serious.

When does your guard go up? When you're with certain family members or at work? When you encounter strangers who trigger your impatience? Revisit these people or these circumstances with a refreshed spirit of joy. Instead of becoming uptight by the quirks and shortcomings of others, find a way to be amused by them. Or at the very least, become informed and wise by observing those weaknesses. Don't do this with a twinge of condescension, but with the peace of grace. A renewed, vulnerable spirit can emerge from behind the walls we've put up to keep us from harm or disappointment.

Let a bit of levity brighten your mood, mindset, and manner. This becomes an act of good will and good nature that ultimately reflects God's love. Amusement will override annoyance. Wonder will outweigh worry. Self-protection will give way to compassion. And through the act of becoming vulnerable and lighthearted, you'll discover a deeper sensitivity to God's leading, wisdom, and will. You'll discover what delights await the heart that welcomes and accepts.

When we show up as our true selves, our conversations with others and our times of silence and laughter shared with others will become our most meaningful, vibrant moments to experience life as prayer.

LIFE Reflections

- When do you shut yourself off or distance yourself emotionally? Try countering that tendency by changing your attitude in advance of those situations.

- Lighten up whenever possible. Add more fun and laughter to your life. Explore one way of "play" today. When you sing, color, have a picnic, swing at the park, or soak your feet in the kiddie pool, you're embracing creative invitations to be vulnerable in the best of ways.

- Delight in your existence by showing up as your authentic self each day. Let that guard down and engage with the life around you. You will shape memories to savor and experiences that make you feel alive.

- Intention: *I will be fully present to someone today. I will be honest about an insecurity to free myself from the hindrance of pride and to open up a relationship with the gift of vulnerability.*

Prayer

Lord, you know how long it's taken me to build up some of my emotional and spiritual walls. Give me the courage and desire to tear them down. I'm tired of peering over the tops of those walls to see what life could be like as someone who walks in peace and lives a prayer of joy. Help me to visualize this new way of being so I recognize it when those walls crumble and you point me in the direction of abundant, whole living.

Joie de Vivre

Take delight in the Lord, and he will give
you the desires of your heart.
PSALM 37:4

Does it seem shameful or indulgent to you to delve into the topics of desire and passion? Have a few misguided romance novels or cable channels caused us to eliminate such words from our language—even when we're talking about our spiritual journeys? What an unfortunate loss! Our spiritual journeys are absolutely, undeniably, unapologetically supposed to be filled with desire and passion. And yet many of us temper our emotions, even when they swell with gratitude for all God is and does in our lives. We walk away from hardship experienced by strangers—and sometimes even friends—because their intense needs remind us of our frailty and deep longings for acceptance and love.

Instead of embracing miracles, we reduce grand, life-changing God-moments to the size of coincidence by rationalizing them with human reason or attributing them to human responsibility. Allow yourself to dive into a glass half full. Believe in the goodness God is producing right now. Your "what-if" worries can melt in the presence of radiant "why-not" possibility.

Joie de vivre, the joy of living, is not reserved for the French, though we could learn a lot from their pursuit of simple pleasures. Don't put out the fires that stir your heart and lead you to impassioned and emboldened faith. Desire leads you to find the One who will shape and fulfill your longing. Passion leads you to gratefully serve the One who seeks to give you the delight of your heart and soul.

LIFE Reflections

- What ignites your passion for living, serving, and being? Step into the "why-not" light and out of the "what-if" shadows. Creativity and joy reside in that brilliant landscape.

- Make the connection between your gifting and your desires. How might the gifts God has given you lead you to fulfill the desires of your heart?

- What longings or joys of childhood did you abandon because they didn't fit the expectations others had for you? Revisit those longings or joys to see if you want to bring one or more back into the home of your heart. Be gentle with yourself. Let this exercise be about the joy of reconnection, not about regret.

- Intention: *I will work "desire" and "passion" back into my spiritual vocabulary.*

Prayer

I want to make the most of this life you've given to me. Let my passions be those you have for me. Show me how to use my gifts—to reveal and use them for godly, fulfilling purposes.

Upon a Star

It seems to me we can never give up longing and wishing
while we are still alive. There are certain things we feel to
be beautiful and good, and we must hunger for them.
GEORGE ELIOT

Stars guided shepherds in the time of Christ. Stars still orient sailors and hikers and help fishermen make their way through the night. Their usefulness is commendable, but their other role makes me a fan. When they wink and glitter against the dark sky, they invite us to speak our hearts. Did you ever close your eyes and wish upon a star for a pink-frosted birthday cake or a chance to meet your favorite singer? The expression of even small hopes is a tender act of faith.

Prayers of adulthood are more wonderful than wishes of childhood because we know who hears these pleas, requests, and expressions of happiness. And we know our wishes don't rise a mere 500 feet in the air and dissipate into the atmosphere. They soar with clarity all the way to the ear of God, and he gladly hears them—whether they are silly or serious, deep or simple.

In the middle of a particularly hard year, I lifted up prayers for simple things, like open parking spaces, sunshine, and afternoons of solitude. God knew I had more important things to pray about because he was the one covering me through the difficulties. Yet as these lighter wishes left my lips, I doubt he was concerned about my shift toward shallow. I believe he had compassion for the woman with her eyes closed and her heart open, who was asking for help to make her way through the day.

Invite God into your day in any way and in any moment you can. Don't edit your wishes and dreams. Enough people in the world want to do that for you. Give life to those sweet ideas that make you smile.

LIFE Reflections

- Keep your connection with the Creator throughout the day by allowing your heart to speak freely and frequently.

- What is your adult equivalent of a pink-frosted birthday cake? Make a wish; say a prayer.

- Receive God's compassion in your life. Your small and big concerns matter deeply to him. He awaits those late-night, whispered prayers.

- Intention: *I'll allow a particular childlike, simple wish to lead me to deeper faith today.*

Prayer

The prayers of my youth were pure and unedited, but I've lost the courage to dream. It's such a loss to stop speaking of my heart's desires and hopes. God, I want to be young in spirit and full of anticipation for what *could* happen. I want to look to you with big eyes and an open heart and share my wonder-stuffed what-ifs and my wild why-nots.

Skipping and Clapping

Some pursue happiness, others create it.

AUTHOR UNKNOWN

Go to any playground, and you'll find a wisdom that surpasses any book learning you've had: the understanding of unadulterated joy. Children aren't taught the ways of joy; it bubbles up from their souls and expresses itself in their broad, welcoming grins and their wide-eyed expressions of awe. Both are usually followed by unaffected laughter.

What I really love is the way children physically throw themselves into life's delight. They don't politely smirk or chuckle. They display physical comedy like they've been training as comedians, but it's even better because it's pure in intention—they're expressing their hearts' bubbling joy. They clap their hands in celebration of puddles, flowers, bugs, or bath bubbles. They smack their lips after tasting something delicious. They hum to music—even when there is no music to be heard. They slap their hands on their short thighs like cowboys after a good campfire joke. And they skip! They half-run, half-dance across a lawn on a Saturday afternoon or down a school hallway to greet a friend.

When did you and I get too big, too old, too tired, too jaded to immerse ourselves in life? I've always been an old soul, but I used to do way more laughing. I'm not really a poised person, but I definitely have shifted toward telling myself more about what I can't do than what I can do. How about you?

Can we get back to that purity somehow? Can we remember our first sips of delight? How sweet. How rich. How fulfilling. And, oh, how we wanted to share it!

LIFE Reflections

- Allow your joy to be shared physically—clap your hands in praise of someone's success or effort, give hugs, smile at your barista and mean it, and, if the situation presents itself, go for the skip. I'm pretty sure even if you don't break out into pure laughter, someone will.

- Throw yourself into something not about gaining success but about gaining joy and a thirst for life.

- Spend some time with a kid or two and model *their* behavior. Let your guard down and follow their lead to experience a bit of time inspired by curiosity, pleasure, and boundless possibility.

- Intention: *I'll introduce joy and affection into the world today with a bit of humor and a well-timed hug for someone in my life.*

Prayer

I've tasted pure joy, but it was a long time ago. When I equate life with routine, rules, and rigidity, remind me how to play and how to be a child of God—savoring delight without shame, self-consciousness, or judgment.

Watching for Your Cue

No matter what happens, keep on beginning and
failing. Each time you fail, start all over again, and
you will grow stronger until you find that you have
accomplished a purpose—not the one you began
with perhaps, but one you will be glad to remember.

ANNE SULLIVAN

The curtain opens to reveal a stage full of musicians sitting with backs straight and bows and hands poised above instruments. The musicians don't scan the audience; they intently watch the conductor and await their cue to play.

And when the music begins, it fills the concert hall with the sounds of grace and light.

When we struggle to live an inspired, creative life, it might be because we're looking to a crowd for approval or permission. Instead of allowing ourselves to do what we love, we take a survey of our closest friends (and critics) or of pop culture to see if our pursuits have merit.

I can tell you—without taking a survey—that your longings have great worth and validity. Go ahead and draw, even if your last picture was of a neon-green cow and a purple, oblong moon. Feel free to write, especially if your eighth-grade English teacher said you lacked imagination. If you were known as the neighborhood klutz, take a few dance spins around the living room. (You can even wear a tutu.) Decorate your bedroom in a color that nurtures you even if it is off-trend. This is living a life of explored beauty.

And when you get stuck in judgment, sit at attention and keep your eyes on the Conductor to await your cue. You will create something of grace and light that could only come from your inspired soul.

LIFE Reflections

- When have you sought someone's permission before exploring an area of interest or passion? How did that turn out?

- Which activities connect you to a sense of God's delight? Create the opportunity for these activities and make them a greater part of your life.

- Become familiar with beauty by seeking it in others and in yourself. Don't become a critic in someone else's life. If you find yourself in that role right now, examine your intentions to discern whether you might be jealous of that person's dream or courage to dream. Embrace that example and go freely in the direction of your own dreams. There won't be room for jealousy in your full heart.

- Intention: *I'll take my cues from God. I won't take my cues from critics and complainers.*

Prayer

God, help me embrace joy. I let today's worries overcome me. I let the questions about tomorrow override my happiness. Lead me to the creative part of me that I've stifled with to-do lists, expectations, and regulations. Help me find the passions you have planted in the deepest part of my soul.

Language of the Soul

Dance is the hidden language of the soul.
MARTHA GRAHAM

Today's a day to get out and move. Become aware of your body and how it connects you to your mind, heart, hopes, and to God. That sounds like an overstatement of benefits, but it isn't. If we consider movement only physical in nature, then we miss out on much joy and wisdom—the very aspects that could inspire you to move more often. Martha Graham said dance is the language of the soul. She wasn't a theologian; she was a dancer. And she experienced the heart's ability to express itself when a person uses rhythm instead of reason and leaps instead of logic.

Moving loosens up the body and then dislodges those stubborn bits of anger, worry, frustration, or grief that can build up when we leave them to sit like stones in the stomach. Many women use their walking time to pray. That's a perfect combination. While our limbs, muscles, and bones join together to send us in a particular direction, our spirits can seek direction from God.

As an observer and introvert, I like to sit and reflect. But when I take time for a walk, I find my creative juices start flowing. Ideas, connections, prayers, answers, and questions bubble up to the surface *and* reverberate throughout my spirit the moment my feet start moving. In *Camino Divina*, an inviting book of walking meditations, author Gina Mammano writes, "I find the things that seem to stick best to my soul and nourish me in simple, slow release are the ones that have a chance to percolate without strict margins of time and expectation."[2]

Take the time to step on out there and experience what percolates in your mind and spirit.

LIFE Reflections

- Find a way to move and a time to move that both allow you to process, create, and pray.

- Avoid the inclination to mask your thoughts with music, podcasts, and audiobooks while you're moving. Take the creative jaunt outside and stay tuned in to what comes up from within and what you experience during your encounter with your chosen environment.

- Your physical forward motion could very well lead to spiritual forward motion. Allow a walk, hike, or other activity to lead you out of your head and into your heart. Pray before you set out and ask God for insight to notice what rises up from your interior.

- Intention: *Today I will breathe in and out while moving my body to loosen up all that has been lodged too long in my heart, mind, and soul.*

Prayer

Speak to me, God. I want to feel your voice inside of me. I want to stop rushing around and start moving intentionally. Give strength to my body and soul as I make adjustments. I want more creativity in my life. I want to be open to your leading. May my thoughts turn to you as soon as I physically move forward with hope and without an agenda.

What You Keep,
What You Give

There is only one real deprivation, I decided
this morning, and that is not to be able to
give one's gifts to those one loves most.
MAY SARTON

We each have gifts we were born with, we grew into, or that have been presented to us during our faith journeys. But the reason we have opportunity, inclination, or ability is not to raise ourselves up or to push forth our personal goals. Those gifts, often uncovered over time and during trials, are meant to be given to others on behalf of God.

What might your gifts be? Hospitality, service, leadership, musicality, influence, sensitivity, creativity, teaching, praying, or caregiving? The list of possibilities is as unique to you as you are. When you're not sure what gifts you have to give, start with the one we all have access to—a willing spirit. From that one gift, you can effect change, influence others, extend a helping hand, or raise the spirits and circumstances of those in need.

It's important, however, to discover your unique gifts. If they are saved and stored, they will form an ever-growing wall between you and your purpose. And there is a good chance that by holding back your authentic strengths, you're holding back a purpose intended to come to fruition. When we use and share our gifts, they lead us to a fuller understanding of God's heart and his intention for our lives. Inspiration and daring acts of being one's self are catalysts for more inspiration and sincerity in the world. We can all look back on times when witnessing the uninhibited passion and effort of someone caused us to commit to something of importance ourselves. If you can't think of an example, then get yourself out to the finish line of a marathon or research the humble beginnings of a humanitarian organization you respect. If your days seem more about deprivation than celebration, observe someone who's living and giving from the depths of their gifting. You will be given a view and a lot of motivation to share from your own well of wonder.

LIFE Reflections

- Struggling to find your gifts? Ask others what they see in you. Take the risk of unraveling the mystery of who you are.

- Have you been storing up your talents? Saving them for a moment of great success? Start using them in ways that grow the servant in you. You'll discover how multifaceted those talents are and how they grow exponentially when they're shared.

- Are you dishonest with people you dearly love about who you are at your core? Consider why you haven't allowed them to see your gifts and flaws. Your vulnerability could invite them to the transparency and healing they need.

- Intention: *I will share my gifts and my honesty with someone I love today without expecting anything in return, including judgment or rejection.*

Prayer

God, fill me with a sense of confidence and strength. When I try to hide behind my wall of insecurities, push me forward through the open gate of your will. When will I start trusting you with my life? All this time of faith, and yet I often move through my days like someone who doesn't know the mercy and might of the Creator. Reveal the gifts and talents within me—then show me how to start giving them away.

Life with a View

Life without faith in something is too narrow a space to live.
GEORGE LANCASTER SPALDING

After much prayer, a middle-aged woman decided to take a long-delayed trip to a foreign city. She arrived at her hotel filled with excitement. She told the manager this trip was answered prayer. His face turned red. "We've misplaced your reservation. Please have a seat while I fix this. I'm so sorry."

"I'm not worried. Whatever room you have is fine. But a view would be so special."

Ten minutes later the manager asked the woman to follow him. They took the elevator to the nineteenth floor. "I think you'll like this view," he said with a broad smile. The woman entered what was clearly the penthouse suite. The manager pointed out the amenities to her, but her eyes were fixed on the glass double doors that framed a breathtaking view of the city square and an exquisite park.

Every morning, the woman sipped coffee on the terrace and planned her outings. She spent evenings full of gratitude looking at the glow of lampposts in the park. On her last evening, she ordered room service so she could savor her beloved view.

The manager himself delivered the meal and asked if she would like him to start a fire in the fireplace. She pulled her glance away from the window and looked at him. "What fireplace?" she asked. His brow furrowed, he took three steps back and opened a set of double doors, revealing a large living area with velvet furniture and a fireplace with a marble mantel.

"Oh, my! I thought those doors led to another closet!"

The manager, clearly appalled, stammered for several seconds, and then said, "It's so terrible! Here you are on your dream trip, and you didn't get to enjoy the riches of it."

The woman laughed, turned back to the window, and sighed. "Oh, yes, I did."

LIFE Reflections

- When one of your dreams is realized, are you quick to note how it's flawed or not quite the way you imagined? Or do you focus on the beauty of the moment and the riches of a new life experience?

- Do you keep raising the bar on what it takes to make you happy? Let the next small joy you encounter invite you to be satisfied. Take in the experience with gratitude and without wishing it was different in any way.

- Has an unmet expectation left you bitter or stuck in a cycle of want? Releasing that expectation to God's care can allow you to move forward with open hands and an open heart.

- Intention: *I will savor the view of my life with appreciation, and I will improve my circumstances simply by being present to the gift of being alive.*

Prayer

God, I have ruined some great experiences by picking them apart when they didn't fit my vision. I catch myself talking about what is not working or thinking through the ways a certain circumstance has not turned out quite "right." I don't want to live with a view of life tainted by regret or from a lack of thankfulness. I want to receive people, situations, changes, possibilities, and even less-than-ideal circumstances with a perspective of hope and love.

Inviting Joy

Don't think so much about who is for or
against you, rather give all your care, that
God be with you in everything you do.
THOMAS À KEMPIS

Build a life with what you have and joy will follow. Our worries tend to center on what won't happen, so much so that we miss out on celebrating what will and does happen. A friend was planning a lovely family gathering. Days in advance, she made preparations for those who would be coming, but her thoughts turned to those who might not show up and why. She knew their presence would be missed and she continued to dwell on them. Soon she was no longer enjoying the process of preparation; her heart had changed focus. Then her husband pointed out a great perspective: When the day comes for the gathering, the ones who show up are the ones to take care of.

How easy it can be to surround ourselves with people we care about and still not emotionally be with them because we're preoccupied with the scenario that will not be, at least not this time. If people stopped offering up themselves and their passions until they had the ultimate turnout or the perfect group, the careers of most musicians would end after one hotel lounge performance. Grassroots organizations would dry up before the mission statement could be read to those who would benefit from its intention. And most ministries would fizzle after one poorly attended Wednesday night meeting.

If we consider each gathering an opportunity for community and connection, then there isn't any good reason to fret over who isn't there. Celebrate, and tend to those God sends to you and those he encourages you to join. At your next gathering, meeting, event, or stuck-elevator incident, look around at the people you are meant to interact with and get to know. Joy is among them.

LIFE Reflections

- Do you focus more on what might not happen than you do on following through with your role?
- Have you pulled back from your purpose because it wasn't unfolding the way you wanted it to?
- Serve those who do show up in your life. Friends and strangers alike are there for a reason, and you're called to show up as well.
- Intention: *I will be there for others, I will invite joy, and I will be grateful for all who show up in my life.*

Prayer

Give me a heart for what does happen and for each person I meet, Lord. When I want to change plans just because they aren't turning out the way I envisioned, give me a new vision and passion for what is unfolding. I will invite faith and joy to be a part of every circumstance and opportunity.

Permission for Possibility

Your life is something opaque, not transparent, as
long as you look at it in an ordinary human way. But
if you hold it up against the light of God's goodness,
it shines and turns transparent, radiant and bright.

ALBERT SCHWEITZER

One day my husband said if something ever happened to him, I should quit my job, sell the house, and move to Paris to live and write for a year or more. I said, "Oh, don't talk like that," and then I said, "Thank you." I liked his dream for me because it suited me. And it meant he was thinking about my passions. Later, I set aside the without-my-husband part of that scenario and took time to ponder what I would do with that possibility. Travel. Write. Purge my belongings. Reevaluate my priorities. Then I considered what I could do with that possibility today, which was each and every one of those things! Yet why don't I?

How are you at pursuing what's on your heart? What leadings drift in and out of your thoughts and prayers and times of silence, even when brief? Is your list similar to mine or radically different? Maybe you're one of the bold and courageous people who have striven to embrace their potential for many years.

All I know is that we need to stop tying our dreams to the anchor of impossibility and start whisking them along with the wings of possibility. God is the creator and fulfiller of endless opportunities, dreams, and visions. We should believe in horizons that open up our lives in ways that surpass our imaginations and hopes. Such experiences are the work of God. His signature is all over brilliant dreams realized. And his hope is behind ordinary dreams brilliantly realized.

I want us to taste that life beyond the excuses. No, I want us to breathe it, embrace it, and ultimately dive headfirst (noses not even plugged) into that life beyond doubt. Not that you need it, but you do hereby have my permission to dream and perceive possibility as a requirement for really living.

LIFE Reflections

- When you're alone with your thoughts and dreams, what are they? What possibility are you longing for? Could today be your prayer of invitation to tend to a dream? Take it for a walk, sit with it at an outdoor café, or give it some journaling time. See what unfolds. It might be your heart.

- Do you give each 24 hours the weight they deserve? They're an entire day's worth of dreaming, living, and being as a child of God. It is significant! Don't trade them for a mediocre passing of time.

- Release your hopes from the anchors of negativity and impossibility. Try out the simple question, "If all my perceived obstacles were cleared for me, what would I be doing right now?" Think about how your answer is an invitation to explore your deepest longings.

- Intention: *I will hold my life up to God and watch it cast streams of light, like a prism, onto my path. I will notice this light around me with new eyes.*

Prayer

Sometimes my hopes feel limited. It's almost as though I've given up on bigger dreams. I want to be alive with excitement and motivation again, God. I renew my hope in your brilliance. I renew my strength in your divine design.

Life as a Prayer for Faith

Daily Sacraments

For everything that lives is holy, life delights in life.
WILLIAM BLAKE

I went to a local restaurant and ordered a basic meal of rice, black beans, veggies, and chicken with a dash of salsa. I gave my name with my order to the manager at the counter, and I retreated to a corner table to wait. A few minutes later, I saw the man step from behind the counter. He called out my name and I stood up to meet him halfway. I reached for my container, and as I did, the manager paused and communicated what my order was. As he carefully listed off the ingredients, they each sounded rich and satisfying. I nodded my thanks, received the cardboard container, and headed out the door to walk several blocks back home. All the while I was thinking about how his presentation of the meal felt like an offering of the sacraments. His manner and our exchange made my ordinary order feel important and personal.

My take-out meal was healthy but it wasn't remotely holy. This sacrament wasn't communion. And yet, this moment of simple generosity and attention illustrated how we can transform ordinary exchanges into meaningful acts of grace. When our manner is deliberate and gentle, we meld the sacred with the everyday. We can do this for others in our lives. For instance, saying grace before dinner will make the time shared over that meal more special. Shaking hands with strangers as we ask their names will make our connections more personal. Asking how someone is and caring about the answer will expand that relationship.

Take time to slow down and have genuine exchanges with people. Whether you're giving or receiving, do so with a grateful heart. And when you can, be sure to list off the ingredients that blend to create your good life. Make this an offering of thanks to God.

LIFE Reflections

- How can you bring the sacred into your daily life?

- When have you witnessed a moment that melded the sacred with the ordinary? How did it make you feel?

- What are your main obstacles to nurturing holiness and goodness? Busyness? Self-importance? Surface living? Uncertain how to begin?

- Intention: *I will enter my day with the word "sacred" on my mind. I will give and receive the daily sacraments of grace and belief.*

Prayer

Show me how to express my awe in your goodness and grace, God. Lead me to seek out ways to honor faith and to serve you. Give me your heart for others so generosity and hospitality become my way of interaction.

Rituals for Life

God is light.
1 JOHN 1:5

Lighting a candle beckons me to sit still. The act is peaceful and inviting, so inviting that my impulse to work, finish tasks, make a call, or roam the house deciding what to do next is extinguished. I have an external focal point that leads to the internal…the soul, the heart. And here I discover, each time, the light of God.

Over the past few years, a spiritual and emotional journey led me back to the practice of lighting a candle to begin a time of focused prayer. To inspire the ritual, I placed a tea light candle in front of a framed image a friend gave me for this journey. It's a beautiful woodcut based on a Gospel story in which Jesus raises a synagogue ruler's daughter from the dead. Above the scene are the Aramaic words *talitha cumi*, which mean "maiden, rise." Beneath the black-and-white contrasted image is the title "Come forth to life." I love that. Isn't that what we all long for? Whether we need joy, hope, mercy, or strength, the steps we take in faith are steps taken toward life. Abundant life. Intentional life. Meaningful life.

My prayers were initially for healing and direction; but over time, as I struck the match and leaned in toward the wick of the tea light candle, many other prayers and thoughts would surface. This simple action reignited a desire to lift up my life completely to God's care.

I don't know what your journey looks like today, but I do know the light of a single candle can help you find your way. It can lead you to times of prayer, meditation, questions, and praises. I invite you to light a candle to honor the mundane and the miraculous, the everyday and the eternal. Paying attention to holy whispers allows us to "come forth to life" in God and in meaningful ways.

LIFE Reflections

- Is your mind scattered? Is your heart divided? Focus them both during your time of meditation and devotion. You might discover that you've been longing for the peace of this simple action.

- Has God asked you to rise and come forth? What do you sense he is calling you toward? Are recent changes possibly preparing space in your life for the resurrection of joy? For purpose?

- How can you embody "sacred"? It isn't about perfection; it's about honoring holiness and being a vessel for God's love. All of life is sacred and mysterious. Enter your day in awe and you will be amazed at what you notice.

- Intention: *Today I will light a candle. It's a simple act, but it will renew my faith and help me see my way forward.*

Prayer

I feel as though I've been asleep for so long. I want to be brought back to life in you. I long to walk forward in the way you have for me without creating self-made detours that become excuses or regrets. I've believed sacredness and holiness are not a part of real life, but I see how each moment is sacred when I give it the weight and value of attention. Give me a deepened sensitivity to the ways you are calling me to full living and full faith.

Missing Peace

God can make you everything you want to be,
but you have to put everything in His hands.

MAHALIA JACKSON

What's missing from your life? Some people respond to this question in one of two extreme ways. One, they build a life around their personal answer. Whether their void is loneliness or value or love, they focus on that one area with such determination that they sacrifice other areas. Or two, they build a life focused on the question itself. They don't know what's missing, but they do know they don't have peace. Their quest to answer the question becomes a singular journey that doesn't lead very far, and the answer is always out of reach.

This question usually sneaks up on us when we face a transition or when we observe someone else's change in season: a new baby, a graduation, a funeral. You might try to shake it off the way you would a tagalong younger sibling, but when you acknowledge what's missing, you can begin to pray for that area daily.

I'm talking a lot about the question and less about the answer because we each have a different void, a different bit of longing that will vary as our life circumstances change. But if we trace the missing piece back to its root—the desire for love, the need for security, the hope of healing—we can rest in the answers we're given by our creator: the guarantee of unconditional love, the assurance of grace, the promise of wholeness.

The peace-filled life is not one large puzzle that requires precisely shaped or colored pieces; the peace-filled life is fluid, beautiful, and abundant. Have you been so focused on getting married or accomplishing a career goal or having a kitchen with green marble tiles that you haven't asked and answered the important question, "Am I ready to let go of the missing piece to have God's peace?"

LIFE Reflections

- Have you pursued one aspect of life with such fervency that you've sacrificed other aspects?

- When do you allow yourself to explore those meaning-of-life thoughts? If the answer is "Never," take time to do that now.

- When do you feel most at peace? Can you allow that sense of God's peace to fill you during other times and amid other circumstances?

- Intention: *I will give all areas of my life to God. I'll do that today, tomorrow, and the next day so it becomes the way I live out my hope.*

Prayer

God, I feel as though I've been missing out on life because of one missing piece. Help me to have hope in this area. Help me turn my focus toward you and all you provide. I give you my concerns, my sense of loss, and my hopes, and I will step into your wholeness and abundance.

Craving God

Prayer is as natural as breathing, as necessary as oxygen.
EDITH SCHAEFFER

Have you ever craved communication with God? This should be our natural state of being! If and when we try to live separately from his breath, nourishment, and power, our existence is a mere shadow of the experience we're intended to have as his creations.

Prayer is our direct connection to God's heart. Without prayer we walk through our days with a concept of God but without communion. We hold God up as deity but risk not embracing him as Healer or Abba. Your need for intimacy with God is as natural as your need for oxygen. Through our relationship with our creator, we are refreshed, revived, and renewed. After we take that first gulp of God's breath into our lungs, we crave it and know we don't want to live without it again. Nor can we.

Your need for the Source—the source that fulfills your needs— never changes. Each day you require that connection all over again. Day in. Day out. When you weep privately over brokenness and pain and know only God's presence will bring healing, you're seeking that connection. When you feel small in the world and call out for direction and meaning, you're seeking that connection. When you feel a craving deep in your spirit and an overwhelming need for God is pressed upon your heart, you have found the source for living. Breathe it in.

LIFE Reflections

- Do you seek connection with God only after you've exhausted your contacts list to meet your needs? Try him first next time.

- Brokenness and gladness alike lead us to God—if we're paying attention. Which are you experiencing now? If paying attention brings up a life prayer of longing, what would you call that longing? If paying attention brings up a life prayer of invitation, what are you being asked to consider?

- What leads you to God? Loneliness, sadness, joy, decisions, conflict, or transition? Embrace any of these as a gift if it redirects your heart to prayer and communion with God.

- Intention: *I'll stop trying to fill my need for God with every-thing and everyone but God.*

Prayer

You're right there, God. Right here. And I still overlook the power of communion, connection, and covenant with you. Help me keep my focus on you so my heart seeks you first in every situation.

An Unfolding Mystery

In all that I value, there is a core of mystery.
MARGE PIERCY

Mystery is tied to faith. That can scare some and intimidate others. But if you consider for one moment how incredibly refreshing it is to not know all the answers, you'll understand the allure of a deep faith that calls you to faithfulness in the times of questioning. A deep faith that calls you to hope in the moments after you leap but before you land. In an age when we can look up any definition, any history, or a ten-year plan for almost anything and everything via the internet, we should embrace the idea of faith. Faith influences our lives. It defines us. It leads us through days that would make us drop to our knees in defeat if we were not already on our knees in prayer.

As much as we study, research, pick apart, and analyze faith, it still beholds the beauty of mystery. This is such a lovely part of belief, and yet we want to feel "in the know" and in control of the information that relates to what we base our life on. That is understandable, but our desire for absolutes undermines the wonder of miracles, and it steals the joy that could be ours for holding on to belief even when we don't know all the answers. Celebrate the unknowns of faith.

If we could pinpoint every single truth of faith, it might make us sought-out scholars. But it would do little to build up our hope in the Lord. The world holds such little potential for mystery and wonder. We are the privileged few—those of us who cling to hope not only in spite of the questions but because of them.

LIFE Reflections

- Have you ever thought about how freeing it is to not know all the answers? Spend time praying about this newly recognized freedom. How might your daily life change once you rest in this freedom?

- When you share faith with others, step away from theology and debate and describe the intimate beauty of faith you have personally experienced.

- What unknown in your life can be viewed as a doorway to hope and possibility?

- Intention: *I will live as someone who believes in miracles and honors the mystery of faith. I will let go of my constant requirement for evidence so I can soak in the wonder that is evident!*

Prayer

Lead me to wonder. When I try to define you and your love, let me rest with the same assurance I have in the aspects of you and your nature I both can and cannot define. Thank you for delighting me with surprises that take my breath away and reminding me of the miracle of life and the wonders of how you work in and through circumstances and people.

Simplicity of Prayer

You can pray while you work. Work doesn't stop
prayer, and prayer doesn't stop work. It requires only
that small raising of mind to his. "I love You, God,
I trust You, I believe in You, I need You now." Small
things like that. They are wonderful prayers.

MOTHER TERESA

Poignant prayers have been scribed over the ages. But such petitions don't soar to heaven more quickly or with greater priority than a simple prayer spoken in the middle of the day while you drive to work, clean a bathroom, or stir-fry vegetables. Well-crafted verses are fine to read when you want to be carried to a mood of meditation and praise, but they aren't necessary for either of those experiences to take place. How it must delight God to hear your musings, questions, and quick words of thanks as you go about your day. These heart-to-heart calls strengthen the bond between the Creator and his creation.

What are your most frequent prayers during a day? "Thank you." "Take this from me." "Help." "Lead me." "Forgive me." "Heal me." "Show me." "Carry me." You can discover a lot about how you relate to God by looking at how many heartfelt calls you make and their nature. You'll also see where the voids are in your communication. If you find you tend to yell for intervention and rarely offer up appreciation, start to expand your gratitude throughout the day. If you praise God and whistle as you work and yet rarely ask for his leading, you might blissfully and blindly be traveling a path that is of your own making.

Make heart-to-heart calls to God a regular part of your day. Don't wait for an illuminated moment of extreme emotion or spiritual awareness. Lift up the small things, the foundation of our lives. They are the gifts you have to offer your God.

LIFE Reflections

- What are your most frequently uttered prayers? Which kind of prayers do you tend to forget about? Try to mix it up. Experience depth in your dialogue with God.

- Pray without an agenda. See what God places on your heart when you stop dictating the conversation's direction. It helps if you take time to breathe deeply and wait on God. Set aside ten minutes to be silent and attentive.

- What are small but essential needs you can lift up as offerings to God today?

- Intention: *When my head takes over my time of prayer, I will stop and let my heart speak.*

Prayer

Forgive me for missing out on the wonders of prayer. I am so quick to offer up my needs that I forget to inquire about the needs of others. Or I forget to lean upon your wisdom and ask for direction as I take both small and big steps forward. May I also learn to hold my tongue so I can feel your hold on my heart.

Faith in Faith

He said to me, "My grace is sufficient for you, for
my power is made perfect in weakness."
2 CORINTHIANS 12:9

It can happen like this: On a Monday you're doing well and feeling secure about life and your place in the world. You pray, you believe, you lean on God. On Wednesday you encounter a sorrow that shakes your foundation of faith. By Saturday you're trying to process your difficult circumstance, regain your balance, and keep on moving in your original direction. But it isn't easy to move forward when you're reaching out to stabilize yourself with every step you take.

It's deeply painful to question God's care or God's presence, but I believe these times of conflict come to many of us. And when they do, having faith might just be the most difficult, perpetual action we can commit to.

What we need to say to those who are experiencing times of doubt and spiritual chaos—and what we personally need to hear when we are struggling—is that it is sufficient to have faith in faith for this time. When your mind is scattered and you spend sleepless nights picking apart everything you believe, from your sense of self to your sense of the Creator, it's okay to turn to and rest in the heart knowledge of faith's power. While we might not believe it during times of sadness or hardship, it's through such storms that we become more certain that God's love is real. He doesn't stand on the other side of the chasm of unbelief and watch you struggle. God is willing to be in the struggle with you, even if you don't understand how grace works, even when you become cynical about the possibility of unconditional love, and especially when you wonder if you have what it takes to trust completely.

You don't have to have all the answers to the questions right now, but you do need one answer. Yes, faith in faith alone is enough for right now.

LIFE Reflections

- How can having faith in faith free you from your burden of uncertainty during hard times? In what part of your life do you most need the comfort and strength of faith right now?

- Do you put too much pressure on yourself to have all the answers—the God-answers of life? You might be trying to replace faith with knowledge and control. Return to faith.

- What struggle have you tried to get through alone? Could this be your invitation to ask God to be in it with you? Consider why this has been hard for you to do in the past.

- Intention: *Through prayer, I will exchange my control, doubt, and pain for the peace of faith. I will do this as often as I need to.*

Prayer

Resting in faith sounds so good to me. My heart has been broken, and I don't understand life right now. Why do I try to figure out everything and fix everything in my own power? I'm tired and uncertain. I have moments of doubt. Give me rest today, God, for today it's enough to have faith in faith.

Powered by Optimism

No pessimist ever discovered the secret of the
stars or sailed an uncharted land, or opened
a new doorway for the human spirit.
HELEN KELLER

If God says "Go," do you take a step back so you can weigh the pros and cons? And do you come up with a whole lot more cons each round? Even people who have the strength of hope and faith find themselves restricted by a attitude of limitation. Along the way many of us learn to fear new things and avoid uncharted territory.

Pessimism causes us to see only a narrow slice of what life is and can be. Chances are God is directing you beyond that narrow slice—and beyond your comfort zone. What good is it to say you rely on the love and guidance of God in one breath and then say no to every opportunity to rely on the love and guidance of God?

When life is going well, we don't want to rock the boat. And when life is a bit rocky, we say, "See, life is hard and unpredictable. I should stick with what is safe right now." This is not a life lived in God's power. This is a life fueled by fear. Commit today to living a life powered by optimism and hope. Reject the voices of the past and even the résumé that shows you've stumbled. After all, those voices and stumbles no longer have power. In you God has created a new life. Live it.

LIFE Reflections

- When have you made choices fueled by fear? Fueled by faith? How are these experiences different?

- List your biggest fears. Face them so they don't sneak up on

you. Don't dwell on them, but pray for the spiritual anti-
dote to those fears. For example, if you fear you will never
be loved, pray to feel the presence of God's love in new
ways. If you fear something bad might happen to you,
pray for protection, but also pray for a deeper reliance on
God—the kind that will carry you when circumstances are
difficult.

- Is forward motion the hardest prayer for you to pray? Has
  that always been the case in your life? Think about a time
  when you opened up to a new path or changed direction
  with faith. What happened?

- Intention: *I'll step out of my comfort zone today to see how big
  life is beyond my limited scope.*

Prayer

My fears blur together. I hardly know what I'm specifically afraid of anymore. I feel uneasy and I often
worry. God, pull me out of this way of thinking and living. I want to rest in your peace and your will. Confidence gained through faith will lead me to a much more
authentic life than one controlled by concern. I trust
you. I lean on you.

Life as a Prayer
for Sanctuary

So Good

Taste and see that the LORD is good. Oh, the
joys of those who take refuge in him!
PSALM 34:8 NLT

It's so good to be here, in this place of refuge. This is the heart of God. Some might mistakenly see God's refuge as a barrier that separates us from the world. They might want it to become a protective wall between our hearts and the harsh times of doubt. But those scenarios aren't examples of godly refuge; they're illustrations of separation and confinement.

God's refuge is a garden with plenty of benches on which to sit and think and pray. God's refuge is an open field where we can walk for miles safely and happily, even when the thunder from storm clouds rumbles above. God's refuge is a gentle valley where we can climb to the top of a hill at night and watch the stars with pure joy and wonder.

I don't think God's refuge has a lot of posted rules. I think when we're in it, when our hearts are longing for communion with God, we're gently nudged in the right direction and lovingly taught the things of goodness and meaning. We see paths with greater understanding, discernment, and clarity. And we see the needs and hearts of others with less judgment and more compassion.

How do you know when you are in God's presence? By the heightened awareness of what is good and life-giving.

LIFE Reflections

- Did you grow up with a lot of rules and very little gentle guidance? It can be difficult to discern the voice of God when we haven't known the voice of love in our human relationships. Consider studying the ways of God's love during your time of meditation.

- Have you ever used the idea of refuge to close yourself off from the world? If you're still there, find a way beyond this self-prescribed gated community. Start living a life of faith out where it can have influence and effect.

- Take time to notice your life. What can you see with more clarity lately? Is God bringing something to the forefront of your spirit? Sit with it in gratitude.

- Intention: *With the goal of freedom, I will tear down this protective wall I built or others built for me.*

Prayer

I could run and run and never reach the limits of your love. I could stare at the sky throughout the night and never see its edges. I find comfort in the limitless expanse of your love and compassion. Teach me to breathe deeply and rest in this freedom. May I recognize what is pure and noble and good in this life.

Leaning into God

Truly, it is in the darkness that one finds the light, so when
we are in sorrow, then this light is nearest of all to us.
MEISTER ECKHART

When we are feeling lonely, afraid, mildly anxious, or anything along the fear spectrum, we want connection with others. But we don't always know how to make that happen. I think the more isolated we are in our emotional state, the more we tend to wait for others to break through to us, to understand our emotional frailty, and to rescue us.

We learn to hold back what could be unsettling to others or might raise an eyebrow if expressed in certain "speak only of good things" company. Many of us have the same problem in our relationship with God. Instead of offering up our needs, we wait for a thundering message to waken us from depression or for an unbelievably great job offer from a stranger we meet in a Starbucks line. Those fantasies aren't nearly as powerful as our act of reaching out to God in our pain or want.

When we reach past our hurt or malaise and connect with others and with God, our vulnerability can usher us into healing. Sometimes a discerning, prayerful friend shows up just when we need her. And sometimes a conversation with a stranger does lead to something amazing. God acts on our behalf all the time. Leaning into God's divine strength and following the light of his leading becomes our nature if we give ourselves to him openly and honestly each day (emotional-mess days included). From those Mondays when we don't want to get out of bed to the days when a great loss leaves us unable to catch our breath, our first action needs to be a conversation with God.

LIFE Reflections

- Is your pattern to wait for help instead of asking for it? Try to be more vulnerable in your communication with others, including with God. Express your doubts and your needs, especially in prayer.

- Did you ever do a "trust fall" at camp or school? Standing, you allow yourself to fall backward, trusting someone behind you to catch you. This is a great visual to have in mind when you pray. Imagine falling back as God catches you and your circumstance every time.

- What are you longing for? Is it provision, direction, courage? Whatever it is, look at your life carefully, then ask yourself if there is evidence that God has been nudging you toward the way to have that longing fulfilled. It's not too late.

- Intention: *Today I will move toward vulnerability with someone I know. And tonight I will pray openly. I will confess my need for God.*

Prayer

I'm learning to be more open about my heartaches and hopes. When I lean into your understanding and strength, I know you catch me each time. God, help me to trust more. Some wounds and wants are deep. Give me the words and faith I need to lift them to your light.

Shaping Space for God

As I started looking, I found more and more.
VALERIE STEELE

In a magazine interview, singer Dolly Parton mentioned that, on all her properties, she has either a chapel or an area with a prie-dieu kneeler so she can take time for prayer and silence during her busy life. I love this idea, and it reminds me of some of my past goals related to making room for God and prayer. For some time I have wanted to create a space in my home for this very thing, but I've put it off. For some time I have wanted to discipline myself to read and reflect on Scripture and journal my responses to it, but I've put it off.

When life throws obstacles in our way or troubles arise, we seek God immediately. We ask for a meeting right then and there. But what about cultivating ongoing, regular sessions with God throughout our day? Wouldn't it be great if our daily habit was to give regularly our hearts and minds and lives over to him no matter what our circumstances?

Don't put off making intentional space for God in your life. Set aside meaningful portions of your day, your heart, and your home and dedicate them to the Spirit's use. These will be places and rituals that usher your heart to God's presence. The more you seek God throughout your day, the more intimately you'll know him.

I'm starting this process with intention and a lot of hope. Today, I will create a time of stillness to savor time with Jesus. Join me?

LIFE Reflections

- Prepare a place of prayer in your life. Make this a meaningful space. Maybe that comfy chair that gets used only when company comes over can be placed near a window for your special spot. Maybe your sanctuary is a walking path along a river. You don't have to sit to meditate and pray.

- Go back to the Sunday school practice of memorizing Scripture verses. Rest in the comfort, inspiration, and peace they offer…that God offers.

- Imagine creating a holy space within. Your heart is that space. What does it look like? What would you add to this interior sanctuary? What would you remove to make it more peaceful?

- Intention: *I will create an external and an internal sanctuary to be in God's presence.*

Prayer

Give me a heart that seeks the refuge of your love automatically. Whether I'm making decisions, facing sickness or struggle, or walking an unplanned course, I will start my journey in your sanctuary. I will praise you as I enter your presence, and I will listen for your leading.

Aware of Prayer

Devote yourselves to prayer with an alert mind
and a thankful heart.
COLOSSIANS 4:2-3 NLT

We quickly offer to pray for others. It's second nature to receive an amazing blessing and confirm that God is good. When our hearts fill with compassion for others, or even for ourselves, we want healing and hope. But it's not always our habit to follow up these kinds of offers, thoughts, and desires with prayer. And why is that? I'll speak of the elephant in the room (someone has to point it out)...prayer doesn't always seem like a real action.

When our prayer lives feel shallow, we're probably tossing out prayers halfheartedly. When our prayer lives feel one-sided, we probably don't want to hear God's part of the conversation. God may be catching a glimpse of our heartfelt needs or our gratitude, but we're missing out on genuine dialogue. Welcome opportunities to pray for others and for your own life. Be grateful for anything that leads you to God's feet. Enter a time of prayer with an alert mind and an alert spirit, ready and waiting to receive God's compassion, love, and healing.

As you light a candle, as you carve out a still, calm moment in the day's perpetual activity, recognize your need for God in and through everything you face. View your life afresh as a prayer. Are you most in need of prayers formed by longing, invitation, forward motion, or the embodiment of God's love? If you aren't sure, ask God to reveal what you need. Then rest in the assurance that insight will be given along with the strength of unconditional love.

Care for your soul with tenderness. It's the most important thing you can do today.

LIFE Reflections

- If prayer feels less than real, figure out what element is missing. Are you truthful when you speak to God? Are you vulnerable? Are you even talking to God, or are you talking *at* God?

- Prayer doesn't require perfection, but it does require participation. Make the effort to be present.

- Alertness doesn't come easy. Give yourself rest, nutrition, exercise, and silence, and see if you are more awake for your times of prayer (and more in tune with your life).

- Intention: *I will start treating the action of prayer with more respect. I will become faithful in this way to experience how reverence gives life to everyday sacred moments.*

Prayer

I will sit with you today, God, because I know you see me, hear me, and know me. I'll sit with you, because there is peace in your presence. I'll sit with you even when the right words don't come to me, because I know you know my heart inside and out. I'll sit with you, because it's time I recognize prayer as one of the most meaningful gifts you created.

Sit with Me

Then Jesus said, "Come to me, all of you who are weary
and carry heavy burdens, and I will give you rest."
MATTHEW 11:28 NLT

Stepping into God's presence is not always easy for me. It's never a question of his whereabouts, but of the location of my thoughts. When I'm ready to be quiet, to be still before God, my thoughts often are of me—and my list of transgressions, mostly. That ever-stinging regret turns a chance for reflection into either a pity party or a guilt trip. So I'm either surrounded by my liveliest, most drastic mishaps, or I'm packing up my baggage and mentally distancing myself. Neither scene ushers me into silence, into focus, or to God's side. I feel I can't enter God's presence with these blatant flaws from my past and the ones fresh from this morning. It seems a bit like joining the queen of England for tea while wearing my favorite sweats—the ones with holes in the knees and hem threads draping like fringe. It's not proper. Pious. Or polite.

Well, here's a big difference: Chances are the queen isn't inviting you or me to tea. But God is inviting us to spend time with him. In the blink of a spiritual background check, he knows about your flaws and that period in your life when you ignored him. And yet the invitation arrives anyway. "Join me," it says. And best of all, it closes with the perfect line, "Come as you are."

LIFE Reflections

- What do you believe you have to achieve, do, or be before you can sit with God? Clear away those human expectations of worthiness and replace them with God's invitation to come to him with all your burdens, flaws, and needs.

- No matter your state of imperfection, are you willing to drop everything and savor the acceptance God gives?

- How and when have you withheld acceptance and love from others or yourself? Spend time in prayer to better understand these specific experiences. Embody God's grace and live it out in your daily life this week. See what happens.

- Intention: *I'll stop making excuses so I can be real before God and experience the wonder of grace.*

Prayer

God, I come with baggage, as you know. Some of it has been an anchor around my heart for a long time. I'll work on giving that over to you, piece by piece. Forgive me for holding back because of my feelings of unworthiness. They keep me from baring my soul. They keep me from your presence.

Landscape of Grace

What would a sinless life look like? I can only imagine.
Strive as I may, I won't achieve it. My interior
landscape is scarred.
CINDY CROSBY

Our eyes grow accustomed to the view from where we stand in life. We know the streets and intersections by heart. We can greet by name many of the people we encounter. Even the people we don't know have familiar faces, and we can nod to them. We know the best routes to our favorite stores, and we slip into "our" spots at church, at work, and at corner coffee shops. This view is consistent. Comfortable. And frankly, it's one we could experience with our eyes closed.

We always need grace. But when we turn to its power with desperation and heart, our view tends to shift from the known to the unknown. We don't recognize the path, and we find little comfort as we maneuver the unfamiliar. But there is grace. It opens our eyes to God's presence and his involvement with our lives. In times of sickness, healing rises. In seasons of despair, hope emerges. In days of fear, peace materializes. In moments of doubt, faith appears.

Be thankful to have your eyes opened to the landscape of grace—it is as vast as the unknown. But in a life dependent on God, it becomes as familiar as the terrain of our own hearts.

LIFE Reflections

- View the unfamiliar terrain as a good thing—an opportunity to shift from independence to total dependence on God. Does the unknown feel like an invitation to keep praying for discernment, or is it meant to be the setting for you to move forward with a change of heart sooner than later?

- Change up your routine. You don't have to wait for a life shift or trial to awaken to the landscape of grace. Step out more. Talk to new people. Take a risk by being vulnerable.

- Comfort is something to be grateful for. But getting too comfortable in life can undermine a sense of gratitude. What can you express thanksgiving for today?

- Intention: *Today I'll resist the temptation to keep life predictable. I will trust God to be with me wherever I am, including when I'm outside my tried-and-true circumstances and paths.*

Prayer

Open my eyes to what I'm supposed to see.

Open my eyes to what I'm supposed to be.

Open my eyes to see the ache in the person before me.

Open my eyes to see the need in this culture of plenty.

Open my eyes to witness healing in the middle of pain.

Open my eyes to see the warm glow of grace cast against the shadow of my complacency.

The Way of the Heart

I wonder sometimes if we haven't banished the way
of the heart in favor of the way of the mind, if we
emphasize learning about God over being with God.

SUE MONK KIDD

Light a candle. Watch the flame. Don't force yourself into thoughts or pressure yourself to come up with the right words to say. When your heart wants to create an offering of a simple prayer, your mind mentions something like how God created Mount Kilimanjaro and gravity, and all of a sudden those words about hope and thanksgiving seem meager and insignificant. When your heart is ready to share its brokenness, your mind weighs the labor involved in healing and wholeness, and you second-guess embarking on the journey. How often do we get in our own way of sweet communion with God?

But when you enter God's presence, you'll feel comforted rather than burdened by the mystery of the unknown. You'll be able to let go of the loud inner-judge and give way to God's grace and acceptance. But you have to leave the way of the world, the way of control and preconceived notions, at the door of your sanctuary, whether it's in a church, a room, or your heart.

Just for once (or even better, try it as a regular habit), let go of your head knowledge about prayer and God. That knowledge is important and useful, and it builds your foundation for faith, but right now, in this moment, let your heart take over. It has amazing things to share with its creator. And it will lead you to sanctuary.

LIFE Reflections

- Let your heart speak. What does it want to say to God? What has prevented you from allowing your heart to speak honestly in the past?

- How often does your mind override your heart and spirit? This week, when your mind takes the spotlight and hijacks your time with God, ask it to settle down, be still, and give your spirit some quality time with its maker!

- When you're with God, be with him fully, wholly, and with an open heart and spirit. After such a session with him, spend time journaling or doodling. What words or images does God place on your heart?

- Intention: *I will make prayer a priority. I will follow the way of the heart straight to God's presence. I won't let my chatty mind interrupt this longing or the flow of prayer.*

Prayer

God, my heart is ready to express its love, its hurts, and its longings. My mind is ready to quit overriding what my heart wants to share and receive. I'm made to have intimacy with you. Thank you for preparing in me that desire for communication and for the peace that comes only from your heart. The gift of sanctuary permeates my life. All I want is to be with you.

Nurtured

The greatest gift of the garden is the
restoration of the five senses.
HANNA RION

Having a sanctuary to go to is a gift. My town has a hilltop garden. When spring comes around each year, this is a tranquil place to wander along pea-gravel paths alongside vibrantly colored rhododendrons that are grand and graceful. Many caring hands and hearts have worked to create such a sacred space, and I am blessed to reap the benefits. At the crest of the hill is a lookout. From here the busyness of life fades to the background and the beauty of life comes to the forefront.

A heart given over to God becomes a sanctuary that, no matter the season, provides a tranquil refuge. Such a sacred space can be created when we allow moments of stillness to become intentional sessions of prayer and reflection, not fleeting intermissions. When we evaluate our lives and weed out the chaos so peace and meaning can grow, we are tending to this inner garden. And when we choose to walk alongside God rather than rush past him with our own agendas and routes, we will see the sights he intends for us to experience.

In reverence and awe, here in the spiritual sanctuary of your heart, take time to revel in God's goodness. Here, the busyness of life fades to the background, the beauty of life comes to the forefront, and you are richly blessed as your senses awaken.

LIFE Reflections

- Quiet is not absence. Stillness is not inaction. Sanctuary is not escape.

- Invite God's goodness to infuse your existence. Only then can you know it intimately. Only then can you share it.

- Even if you don't run around with your every move planned, chances are you live by your own agenda. Try to give that over to God this week. Leave space for what God might be offering you. It might be rest, a conversation, an idea, or a prayer. Only God knows!

- Intention: *I am a blessed child of God. I'll walk forward in this identity rather than one shaped by my success, performance, or goals.*

Prayer

I don't always see the weeds that crop up in my habits and plans. God, point out those activities, thoughts, and expectations that don't belong in the sanctuary you've planned for me. Give me the discernment and discipline to rid my life of them. I want to make room for the flowers of hope and the potential you plant alongside my journey's road.

Strong Connection

Only when one is connected to one's inner core is
one connected to others. And, for me, the core, the
inner spring, can best be re-found through solitude.
ANNE MORROW LINDBERGH

Much value is in the sacred act of creating space and resting in solitude. Not so we can distance ourselves from community and covenant with others, but so we can take time to restore our sense of peace and belonging as God's children. Does the idea of solitude make your palms sweat and your mind flit and flutter with ways to sabotage any blip of stillness? If this kind of internal activity occurs for you, direct it as an offering to God. Lift up your weary heart or specific praises and petitions. Abba graciously receives these and will embrace you with assurances and peace.

When I take advantage of solitude to seek God's heart, I'm renewing my sense of connection with every person on earth. When I light a candle and lift up the prayer that has gone unspoken for days because I've been too distracted or self-centered, I experience renewal, hope, and sensitivity toward others.

We can walk among the masses and feel lonely, but as we enter God's presence, we are no longer isolated in our thoughts. We are given the security of his very real attention and love, and we are guided to notice that we're a part of something so much bigger than our current concern. And then something wonderful happens within the core of our spiritual self…we see beyond ourselves.

As much as I lean toward being a loner, I know this can never be my identity. I get chills as soon as I slip into God's presence and think about how interconnected my life is with that of the stranger I passed at the coffee shop or the best friend I've had since high school. This is the body of Christ. I'm a part of it. You're a part of it.

LIFE Reflections

- Does the idea of turning to solitude to understand your part in something bigger than yourself seem like an awkward paradox? Allow yourself ten minutes of prayer and reflection today. Does this solitude lead you to a sense of solidarity with God and others?

- Your time in solitude does not have to be in silence. Choose inspiring music for your time alone. Bake something. Whistle. Journal. Just let your thoughts be of and for God.

- Consider asking a friend to set aside the same time of day you will to be "alone" in God's presence. Later, share with each other what it felt like to join in the practice simultaneously.

- Intention: *I'll figure out how to dedicate some of my alone time to seeing and seeking God. I'll make notes. I'll savor the images and have them impressed on my spirit and heart for future reference.*

Prayer

Calm the pace of my heartbeat. Steady my thoughts. Ready my spirit. I want to experience your presence, God. I don't want to feel lonely anymore or alone in my life. People, good people, let me down because they couldn't be—and cannot be—everything to me and everything I need. Grant me the wisdom to turn to you as my source for all. Then when I share my time and self with people, it can be from the steady place of peace.

Light Therapy

For light I go directly to the Source of
light, not to any of the reflections.
PEACE PILGRIM

When you're light deprived, your body hungers for it. I live in a region that has some pleasant months but also has a long rainy season. It's easy for my moods to follow the way of weather patterns, so I bought a special blue light that emulates sunshine and produces similar good effects in the body and mind. All that's required? I sit with the gentle blue rays beaming in my direction for 15 to 30 minutes each morning. What a worthwhile trade-off for an improved mood and better sleep.

Our spirits need light too. We crave the warmth of God's light. It offers nourishment and comfort. It fills us with hope and energy to press on. Imagine how much better our lives can be when we make a commitment to spend 15 minutes a day basking in God's light. It will improve our demeanor, outlook, attitude, perspective, motives, heart, and our sense of joy.

Do you take time to let in the light? Are you in actual spiritual darkness, spending your days under a cloud of depression, sadness, or loneliness? I believe many of us and many of the people in our lives experience the negative side effects of insufficient illumination. We need the radiance of promises, hope, and love. How do you seek the Source? Explore Scripture verses that speak to your current needs. Light your candle and close your eyes and pray. Not sure what to say? Ask for joy. Ask to become a reflection of God's brilliance. Discover how to radiate the love God gives you every day (well beyond a 15-minute session).

No need to flip a switch. Just turn over a new leaf, perhaps. Today is the day you can seek God's light, and experience the lasting joy of everlasting love.

LIFE Reflections

- Have you lost the luster of a vibrant faith? Have you become dull in mind and spirit? When your thoughts are self-focused and every day is the same because you distance yourself from the spark of inspiration, you're ready for light therapy.

- For best results, place God's light at heart level. Studying about God is good, but to embrace the joy of Christ you need to direct the light of God's love at your heart. Does this light reveal a longing? Does light on the path ahead illuminate an invitation?

- What brought you joy when you were younger? Bring a version of that back into your life. Ask God to introduce you to new ways of spiritual and personal refreshment.

- Intention: *I'll go to the light of God today to refuel, restore, and renew my sense of joy.*

Prayer

How have I lived in such darkness for so long, God? I want the light back in my life. Show me the way out of the shadows. May the covering of fear be lifted so my spirit is drawn to and nurtured by radiant light. Give me the courage to recognize the shadows that reside in me so I can examine them and hold them up to the radiance of grace.

Life as a Prayer
for Purpose

Your Heart Will Follow

Trust in what you love, continue to do it, and
it will take you where you need to go.
NATALIE GOLDBERG

When our lives are driven by immediate needs rather than eternal hope, we become stuck, thrown, lost, or flat-out exhausted. And when that happens, all we want is a superlong nap. Four days long would be ideal, but if you'll settle for a few catnaps and some times of prayer, I believe you'll be ready for this next step.

Start moving forward. You might not feel motivated or ready, but if you've become complacent or disheartened, you can still get the momentum going. Have you experienced loss in your life? Reflect on that void, and then ask God to fill it up with his healing and renewal. If your job is dissatisfying or is consuming all your energy, make time for activities you love—they could very well lead you to greater purpose. Is the weight of the world on your shoulders lately? Ease up on watching the news and take a break from filling your mind with images and sound bites. Calm your spirit and pray without distraction—feel God's peace. If you lack motivation, yet desire to make a lasting change, seek accountability with others and commit to lifting up that area of your life in prayer daily.

It isn't always easy to break loose during times of stagnation, but it is time to live life like never before. Your life matters, and this day in your life matters. Move forward today. Either a baby step or a big leap will send you on your way—and your heart will follow.

LIFE Reflections

- Move forward—stop being stuck. Complacency or bitterness will set in if you don't give yourself over to God's momentum.

- Figure out what you need accountability for in your life so you can make lasting change. Set up a system of checks and balances with friends or set meaningful goals.

- Breathe calm into your life little by little. Choose a time each day to breathe deeply and exhale with steadiness for several minutes. Eventually this can become your go-to boost during the day. It's life-giving!

- Intention: *I will show God the void in my heart so he can fill it with light and love.*

Prayer

I'll follow you today, God. I'll make room for you. I'll stop rushing ahead with my expectations and demands, because they lead me to only more frustration and life noise. Help me to listen for the still, small voice within. Where are you taking me today? That is what I will ask each morning. And then my heart and I will follow.

Happy with the Present

Happiness is not a state to arrive at,
but a manner of traveling.
MARGARET LEE RUNBECK

We can experience great relief when we stop dictating what will give us happiness and allow God to gently, or sometimes swiftly, move us toward true contentment. Probably, as many definitions of happiness exist as there are people. But many of us define joy in terms of something we hope will happen in the future. "I would be so happy, if I got that job." "Life would be so wonderful if I didn't have so much responsibility right now." "Once I retire the good life will begin!" "When my kids are older, I'll be able to figure out what I want my life to be."

It's fine to hope for change or for things to be different, but if these future versions of life become our only examples of joy, we'll never find the happiness God has placed all around us in our immediate circumstances. Like buried treasures, they lie hidden in the people, conversations, decisions, and possibilities we encounter daily but don't recognize. A life spent immersed in negatives doesn't accumulate faith. So don't let the possible troubles or the circumstances that feel limiting stop you from discovering what could be. You're just stuck, and it's time to imagine moving through life with hope. I would also guess it's time to travel with a bit less baggage.

If you are hard-pressed to find blessings and delight in your current circumstances, don't pray for God to fast-forward you to a new scenario; pray for him to reveal those hidden treasures that exist now as you move forward in life with faith.

LIFE Reflections

- Stop waiting for happiness to come to you. Discover it in your present life.

- Consider how you've defined happiness over the years. Was that standard handed down to you by parents, by a sense of competition, by career standards, or by something else? Be sure you aren't borrowing someone else's version of delight while you miss your daily opportunities to experience deep joy and satisfaction.

- How have excuses served you in the past? Did they protect you from having to trust God? Did they keep you from taking a chance on trying something new? Pray to release those excuses, and then to be released from the grip of those long-held, self-imposed limits.

- Intention: *I will base my happiness on the security of God's love and his desire for me to know the fullness of joy.*

Prayer

God, why have I adopted such an unattainable version of happiness as my standard? I want to stop selling my life short. I want to know the depths of happiness. Help me to become a person who creates joy and invites others to join in.

Declare Your Dreams

Each of us has an inner dream that we can unfold
if we will just have the courage to admit what it is.
And the faith to trust our own admission.
The admitting is often very difficult.

JULIA CAMERON

Has God given you a dream that makes you smile when you think of it? What keeps you from realizing it? It's easy to stifle a dream by holding it too close. Share it, and it will have the space to grow. If the dream doesn't seem complete in your mind's eye, you're probably right. Most great ideas present the initial impetus for something bigger. The missing pieces will come into view once you put that dream out into the world. You might have half of an idea, and then someone you meet in three months might have the other half. Or something you are going to learn in the near future might give your dream more dimension and direction. The lesson God gives you today might be in preparation for the fulfillment of this dream.

Do you have gifts and talents you'd like to use more often? Do you feel the tug to step into a leadership role with a ministry or an organization that touches your heart? Have you walked by a house in your neighborhood numerous times and wished you had the guts to introduce yourself to the woman who lives there? Your dream might be as simple as finding a friend or as involved as starting a business. Small or big, dreams begin with the courage to recognize what God is building in your heart. Declare those dreams. They will unfold when you confess them as a possibility!

LIFE Reflections

- Make a mental list of your hopes. Choose one or two and then reveal your "secret" to a mentor, to a group of girl-friends, or to your spouse.

- See how the people you encounter and the things you learn today could relate to the dream God has placed on your heart. Be attentive to the unfolding!

- Shake up your dreaming. Give yourself time to explore those happy thoughts you may have buried under old obligations or expectations. Plan to sit in a comfy chair or on a garden bench with a sketch pad or journal for a 30-minute personal brainstorming session. List what gives you joy or makes you smile. List what gives you peace. Nothing is too silly or too serious when you're getting reacquainted with your heart.

- Intention: *Today I will watch as God shapes my dreams and brings new ones before me.*

Prayer

Help me see how you are working in my life and the lives of others. I will give you praise for this journey I'm on because I'm dependent upon you and your strength. I'll never know what tomorrow holds, but I do know you are here with me, that you see the big picture, and that you knew of me and my life before I even existed. I can't wait to see how the dreams you give me become experiences that lead me closer to your heart.

Anywhere but Here

There is no need to go to India or anywhere else to
find peace. You will find that deep place of silence right
in your room, your garden or even your bathtub.
ELISABETH KÜBLER-ROSS

This can't possibly be where God wants me!" Do you ever think this? Do you look around and wonder how you ended up "here"—a place in life and time that falls short of your dreams or goals? Or maybe you've achieved your aspirations, but they haven't offered the fulfillment they promised when they were far off in the distance, dangling before you like a carrot.

We can find disappointment anywhere, including where we aren't. I wish settling into our purpose was merely a matter of gathering up our belongings, sending out change-of-address cards, and carting furniture, a few books, and a favorite lamp to another location. But that would be trying to force a physical answer to address the spiritual question, "How can I find contentment and meaning in my current life and circumstance?"

First, we need to stop looking "elsewhere," because that leads us to deceive ourselves into believing happiness can materialize only somewhere else. It also causes us to stop believing in God's amazing power to change our lives and perspectives. Next, we need to look to where there is contentment and meaning—in God's peace and will. And last, we need to take our discouragement or apathy—or whatever it is that first caused us to doubt—to God and watch him turn it into something useful for our journey of purpose: hope, understanding, discernment, grace, peace, anticipation, or wonder.

LIFE Reflections

- Seek refuge in your own life for a while. Give yourself the gift of time and nurturing.

- Light a candle, say a prayer, and step into rituals that breathe life back into your day. Renew your sensitivity to God's gentle leading.

- What version of life do you pine for? Start investing in what's going on here and now. Things can and will change, but not if you stop working on your life as it is.

- Intention: *I will see the wonder of my life right now. I will give each day to God as an offering and make the most of every moment.*

Prayer

When my hopes became a long list of wants that left me feeling dissatisfied, they stopped being a part of my faith. They became excuses for me to complain. You have shown me dreams can inspire my daily living in a healthy way when I give those dreams to you. Please give me a heart for the things you want to be a part of my life.

Awaiting Transformation

What counts is whether we have been transformed into
a new creation. May God's peace and mercy be upon all
who live by this principle; they are the new people of God.
GALATIANS 6:15-16 NLT

A restless spirit can cause us to question what we are doing and why we're doing it. Have you experienced that kind of inner agitation and not been sure why? Restlessness can creep upon us when life is going along as planned. It can emerge when we're in between milestones and living life in a holding pattern. The restlessness can feel like crisis to some and like awakening to others.

If you've had a season of trial or endurance that has left you weak and weary, the restlessness could be from a spirit that has yet to return to trust. Or maybe your body and mind truly need long stretches of sleep and silence. Don't deny yourself this self-care and love. God can hold you and hold down the fort of your life while giving you nourishment for physical and spiritual renewal.

You might be on the other side of a trial when hunger arises or uncertainties flood your normally steadfast thoughts. When this happens, you might be inclined to doubt everything, but it is the perfect time to believe in what God is preparing in your heart and spirit. Those stirrings are possibly the birthing pains of wonder and growth. God is preparing you for a trial, a change, an epiphany, a ministry, or a deeper level of faith. Sit with the uneasiness and the anticipation. During this time of awareness, pray for direction, thank God for the unknown, and prepare to experience life and faith differently. View the shift in your spirit as a gift, even if it's uncomfortable.

Are you more unsure about life than ever before? Welcome to the beginning of your transformation.

LIFE Reflections

- What triggers your uneasiness? What do you usually do to avoid exploring the root of it?

- Consider journaling through this time. Ask yourself what the invitation from God in the midst of the uneasiness might be. Then spend time writing down promises and truths that bring peace to your troubled heart. Now speak them aloud.

- Awakenings are not just for other people! Be a witness to all God is calling you toward these days. And don't look behind you to see who the goodness and blessings are headed for; they are coming your way.

- Intention: *I will let hunger lead me back to God for answers. It will be both my invitation and my forward-motion prayer.*

Prayer

I feel as though my soul is pacing as it waits for something new, something meaningful to take shape. I've felt this before, but I've tried to ignore it by revving up my external activity. I don't want to be afraid of hunger and longing, because they lead me to you. Direct me and my next steps.

Nothing Too Great

All we are asked to bear we can bear. That is a
law of the spiritual life. The only hindrance to the
working of this law, as of all benign laws, is fear.
ELIZABETH GOUDGE

After some years of expending significant energy, time, and effort toward one area of life, I feel weary. Have you been through a season of depletion? Did you lose hope or love? Physically, such a time is demanding. You crave heavy sleep that carries you through dream after dream, yet rest comes only in fits and starts. Spiritually, such a time is distancing. You want connection to God, yet intimacy is elusive.

These times of emptiness become experiences of healing and peace. God longs for us to be whole and complete. Our circumstances may have taken away something of great importance, but when we offer our hearts to God as empty, hurting vessels, he fills them until they can hold no more. Healing can be painful. As peace pours back into our lives, it will stretch our hearts and dreams. We have to relearn what it feels like to be replete with God's love and satiated with the sweetness of hope.

When you spend sleepless nights and difficult days measuring your emptiness, don't worry that its dimensions are too great for your human efforts to ever fill. No pain or weariness is too big to be brought to the Source of your joy and healing. God's mercy will keep on flowing until pain is replaced by peace and your loneliness is replaced by lasting communion.

LIFE Reflections

• Do you believe God is greater than the hurt you feel?

- When has fear pulled you back into the emptiness? What did you do? How have you broken through that fear? Or does that fear still rule your emotions and dictate your opportunities?

- What do you hope for in God? Healing, rest, peace, answers, forgiveness? He offers all of these to you. Wait with anticipation to see how you will be given strength to embody these longings.

- Intention: *I will let go of the physical or spiritual trial that has emptied my heart and ask to be filled with hope.*

Prayer

Fill me with your love, God. Replace the ache of pain with the ease of peace. I've held back my hurt because I saw no way around it or through it. You are that way. Lead me into your mercy.

Borrowed Longings

The really important things are not houses
and lands, stocks and bonds, automobiles and
real estate, but friendships, trust, confidence,
empathy, mercy, love and faith.
BERTRAND RUSSELL

Our moods, priorities, and decisions can be swayed by an important factor. I'm not talking about our diet or finances. I'm looking at a more internal force: our longings. What are you striving to accomplish or become? Do you crave attention and love? Have you always wanted a large family? Do you long for a big house with a perfect yard? Some days, do you wish you were in a different marriage or a new family altogether?

Longings can draw us closer to our purpose if they are directed toward God. When our hearts long for God's love and for his grace to sweep over our lives, we are looking for healing and a chance to belong. But when our longings become a persistent grumble, one long sigh of dissatisfaction, they are no longer tied to our dreams and purpose but are anchored to malcontent and the world's sense of fulfillment and entitlement. In fact, I think more than a few of us are carrying a sense of regret or envy over things that aren't even our longings to begin with. We listen to the expressed dissatisfaction of our peers, coworkers, celebrities, or friends, and soon our lives, which seemed fine the day before, are cast in a gloomy shade of gray. This is when we truly believe life would be better, if not perfect, in that house, with that spouse, with those clothes, in that car, near that beach, or in that dress size.

Notice where daydreams take your heart and be willing to go deeper. When you're frustrated about a situation or a relationship, consider whether you are measuring it against someone else's version of the good life. Redirect your longings toward the things of God—compassion, love, patience, perseverance, kindness, and integrity. These desires will not mislead you. They will fill your life and satisfy your heart.

LIFE Reflections

- Whose longings are you striving to fulfill? Have you borrowed a few from parents, from friends, from our culture? Which borrowed longings are you ready to let go?

- Which godly longings would you like to focus on? Choose one way to move forward from longing to action.

- What has caused you a sense of dissatisfaction lately? What invitation might there be in that circumstance? Evaluate whether your emotional response is triggered because you are comparing your life to someone else's situation.

- Intention: *I will pursue the dreams that have my name on them—the dreams shaped for me by a personal God.*

Prayer

I've realized I live my life with a twinge of discontentment because I'm pursuing what has nothing to do with my purpose. God, give me a peace for those pursuits that are of you and your direction for me.

The Beauty of Resurrection

Often, in the midst of great problems, we
stop short of the real blessing God has for
us, which is a fresh vision of who He is.
ANNE GRAHAM LOTZ

At one time in our lives, life changed for you and me. Losses left gaps in our dreams and swayed our paths with such force that we never quite got back on track. Many of us have spent a lifetime trying to retrieve what went missing so long ago. Whatever we have lost through mistakes, brokenness, pain, illness, or rejection leaves us with a picture of "what could have been" had those sufferings never occurred. Retrieval involves a constant desire to re-create what we had just before life shifted. Just before we lost our way. Just before we reluctantly changed our plans and dreams.

Don't confuse the human instinct of retrieval with the divine intention of resurrection. Retrieval works double-time to reestablish what was. It's a painstaking, detailed effort to put everything back in its place just so. But resurrection is God's life-giving force. It doesn't strive to repeat life, because that would take away from the power loss can bring when we understand its nature. Resurrection seeks to find what will be—what can be—because of a void, a hunger, a sorrow. It doesn't try to piece together a shabby version of an old life, because it's designed to nurture, create, and establish something new. It uses the materials found in the aftermath of loss, but it never tries to return to life as it was before that loss.

No power exists in those remnants you hold in your hand so tightly. Grab on to the life being created in you now. You have a new vision of life and a truer understanding of God's love and care. Beauty and meaning can come of loss if we don't try to re-create what's old, but prepare ourselves to embrace a new life.

LIFE Reflections

- Have you invested more belief in retrieval than in resurrection?

- Do you want what replicates the past? Or what transcends what is known and offers rebirth? How can you move toward the latter?

- The life lived in the power of Christ's resurrection doesn't mourn the small deaths of circumstances and seasons. This is a life that sees beginnings and restoration with each change.

- Intention: *I'll release my hold on those remnants of past dreams or broken paths, and I'll reach out for the beauty of a new vision, a new truth.*

Prayer

I really want to live in the power of the resurrection, Lord. I believe in transformation and a life renewed and changed by your grace. Rather than try to control that power of the resurrection by seeking to retrieve what's lost, I will let go. Then I can experience what can unfold through your grace.

Get Dancing

Life is either a daring adventure or nothing.
HELEN KELLER

Maneuvering life is hard. Learning to take the right steps and make the correct moves can trip us up at any point. Even when I think I've memorized good instruction, I've jammed my big toe and I've leapt when I should have bowed. I have always been a closet learner, wanting to master something on my own, away from possible evaluation and scrutiny.

Do you prefer to carefully orchestrate how you learn and when you learn, and determine when you feel ready to try something under the gaze of another? The shocking and embarrassing (and freeing) truth is that most of the time nobody is watching. But if we focus on ourselves long enough, we don't notice that no one is watching. It isn't that people don't care; they just happen to have better things to do. Or maybe they're focused on themselves and not the woman trying to knit in public for the first time or the person working up the courage to dine alone at a local bistro.

We command joy out of our lives when we place ourselves in charge of the learning curve. When we say no to opportunities that take us by surprise, we miss out on God's leading. You aren't the designer of your life. You make choices, and you can refuse to open up to possible failure and public ridicule, but you have to release control to God. When you or I limit the number of times we're willing to try, we're also placing a limit on how often we'll trust God.

Where's the joy in that life?

We should learn something daring together. How about juggling fire, kayaking in level 5 rapids, or something as radical as making a basic, unpracticed dance move in public? That first demonstration of faith and freedom could lead us to some amazing next steps.

LIFE Reflections

- What have you been putting off for years because you haven't wanted to risk failure?

- Build up the courage of a friend today by encouraging his or her dreams and opportunities.

- Risk your heart a little, risk your pride a lot, and move forward in ways that serve your spirit of joy and somehow serve others.

- Intention: *I will step beyond my comfort perimeter today and try something new. I will focus on the joy of being brave in the moment and not on my predicted outcome.*

Prayer

God, I claim to have faith, and yet I hold back from walking in that faith. Where is my trust in your support and leading? Give me courage. Help me break through my hesitation, excuses, and pride to see the joy in taking leaps of faith and delighting in a life without limits.

What to Pack for Time Travel

Lives based on having are less free than
lives based on either doing or being.
WILLIAM JAMES

It's midnight and I await 12:01 to mark the start of a new year. Straddling two years makes me feel like a time traveler. I hear fireworks. I always wonder who sends those lights and sounds skyward for the holiday. And yet on many eves I've been in the REM state of slumber when the actual changeover from old to new has taken place. I never thought I missed out on much, but I was wrong. When I stay awake and ponder what it means to begin again, I discover a great sense of optimism. Who are we if not beings who like beginnings? We don't always enjoy the work involved with starting over, but the appeal of a fresh start is strong for most of us.

Make the most of a new day. Apply a rush of optimism to aspects of your life that are staid and stagnant. If you're standing on the dividing line between what is past and what can be, how do you hope things will be different as you step fully into the present and set your sights on the future? What or whom should you let go? I like to examine what I should pare away from my attitude (sarcasm, apathy) and my possessions (clothes, unused workout equipment). Then it's fruitful to prayerfully consider what I should be adding to my life in the form of activities (volunteer opportunities), concerns (community health care), and dreams (travel, write).

Life is precious. Don't wait for the transition to a new year to consider what you can get rid of, what you are lacking, and what you are grateful for. Every morning you are traveling through time; it just happens to be through your today. Carry with you only what matters. And don't regret leaving a few things in the care of yesterday.

LIFE Reflections

- Think of one of your beginnings and how much it added to your life. What did it lead to?

- Do you straddle yesterday and today? Make the jump to today and see what you can do when your priorities and sensibilities are not divided.

- What do you think God wants you to leave behind? What are you supposed to take with you as you move forward?

- Intention: *I'll make a fresh start today and embrace the possibility of possibility!*

Prayer

This or that? That or this? God, help me decide what to take with me as I press on toward possibility. Fill me with the light of optimism. I want to cherish my time, I want to savor my life, and I want to live the gift of today.

Notes

1. Parker J. Palmer, *Let Your Life Speak: Listening for the Voice of Vocation* (San Francisco, CA: Jossey-Bass, 1999), p.55.

2. Gina Marie Mammano, *Camino Divina—Walking the Divine Way: A Book of Moving Meditations with Likely and Unlikely Saints* (Woodstock, VT: Skylight Paths, 2016), p. xiv.

Acknowledgments

I am grateful for the support and kindness of many. I want to thank...

The Willamette team at Harvest House for their hard work and ongoing efforts on behalf of my writings and those of many others, especially LaRae, Betty (you are always in my corner!), Shelby, Kathleen, Amber, Karri J., Aaron, and Christianne.

Brad and Ken, for catching the vision of this book and helping it find its way into selling venues and ultimately into readers' hands.

The generous spirits who are aplenty in my life. A shout out to Cara (text me).

My sister, Dawn, who saves me in so many ways, and the sisterhood duo of Carolyn and Mimi.

My spiritual direction teachers Ravi and Christopher and my fabulous cohort, the Scary Precious, who are truly far more precious than scary. I am grateful for each one of you.

My nephew Ben, who is the easiest person in this world for me to faithfully pray for and over.

Mom and Dad, for your ever-present love and support. My dear Marc for these years of partnership as we figure out life...and to my Lyda family.

And special thanks to my friend Kimberly Shumate for her keen organizational and editorial touch for this project, and for her example as a woman who walks, breathes, shares, and lives prayer.